**Chris**
www.cl

Mission Statement:
"To help build the Kingdom of God here on earth — one Christ-centered business at a time."

You are about to be exposed to ideas that can change your spiritual life, family life, and business life. The Christian Entrepreneur Steps are designed to teach you the process of spiritually incubating your business idea, writing your business plan, and opening your new business.

## The Christian Entrepreneur Steps

Step One — Realizing God's calling to start a business.

Step Two — Attend The Christian Entrepreneur, Build a Christ-Centered Business seminar to learn Biblical wisdom about finances and business.

Step Three — Write a rough draft of your business plan.

Step Four — Bring your draft to The Christian Entrepreneur Boot Camp to get feedback from a small group of your peers about your business idea and plan.

Step Five — Complete the final draft of your business plan and take it to a Small Business Development Center or Score (www.score.org) chapter in your area for a final critique.

Step Six — Consider joining The Christian Entrepreneur Club for continuing information about building a Christ-centered business and to be among like-minded people.

Step Seven — Start your business! Avoid analysis paralysis!

*Visit our website to get the latest information about building a Christ-centered business.*

ISBN: 1-892669-57-9 (trade paperback)

ISBN: 1-892669-58-7 (ebook)


Copyright © 2011 by Bruce Richard Gehweiler. All rights reserved.

Published by;
Marietta Publishing
677 Valleyside Drive
Dallas, GA 30157
Contact brucegmp@yahoo.com for bulk orders of this title.

Graphic Designer: Rich Harvey

No part of this publication may be reproduced, stored in a retrieval system, or transmitted in any form by any means, electronic, mechanical, photocopying, recording, scanning or otherwise, except as permitted under Section 107 and 108 of the 1976 United States Copyright Act, without either the prior written permission of the Publisher, or authorization through payment of the appropriate per-copy fee to the Copyright Clearance Center Inc., 222 Rosewood Drive, Danvers, MA 10923, 978-750-8400, fax 978-646-8600, or on the web at brucegmp@yahoo.com. Requests to the Publisher for permission should be addressed to the Permissions Department, Marietta Publishing, 677 Valleyside Drive, Dallas, GA 30157.

Limit of Liability/Disclaimer of Warranty: While the Publisher and the Author have used their best efforts in preparing this book, they make no representations or warranties with respect to the accuracy or completeness of the contents of this book and specifically disclaim any implied warranties of merchantability or fitness for a particular purpose. No warranty may be created or extended by sales representatives or written sales materials. The advice and strategies contained herein may not be suitable for your situation. The Publisher and Author are not engaged in rendering professional services, and you should consult a professional where appropriate. Neither the Publisher nor the Author shall be liable for any loss of profit or any other commercial damages, including but not limited to special, incidental, or other damages. Every concept, method form, and entitlement contained herein are the property of this work's copyright holder.

Scripture Quotes copyright © 1965, 1987 by Zondervan Corporation, the Amplified Bible or © 1977 by the Lockman Foundation, the New American Standard Bible. Used by permission.

Printed in the United States of America

*The*
# Christian Entrepreneur

*Build a Christ-Centered Business*

**Pursuing the American Dream of Business Ownership through Christ**

# Bruce Gehweiler

*Founder of the
Christian Entrepreneur Club*

Marietta Publishing
Georgia, USA

This book is dedicated to

*Byron Chiger*

A real friend through thick and thin since 1984 and the person I have learned more about Christianity from than anyone else. Every day is a celebration of the love of Christ because you taught me how.

# Contents

**Introduction — God's Business Wisdom** ............................................. 9
**Chapter One—The Christ-Centered Business**
    The Enlightened Business ............................................................. 13
    God's Will for Your Life ................................................................. 15
    Enlightened Business Verses Greed ............................................ 16
    Converting an Existing Business .................................................. 18
    Portable ......................................................................................... 20
    A Call to Action ............................................................................. 21
    Executive Summary ..................................................................... 22
**Chapter Two—Leadership**
    Preparing for Leadership ............................................................. 24
    Nine Habits of an Enlightened Business Leader ......................... 27
    Executive Summary ..................................................................... 30
**Chapter Three—The Art of the Start**
    Start Here ...................................................................................... 31
    The Odds of Success .................................................................. 32
    Successful Business Defined ...................................................... 32
    Franchising ................................................................................... 33
    Personal Financial Strength ......................................................... 33
    Christian Entrepreneur Profile—Truett Cathy ............................... 34
    Executive Summary ..................................................................... 37
**Chapter Four—Biblical Teachings about Money**
    Choosing the Wealth Path ........................................................... 38
    Poor Money Decisions ................................................................. 38
    Consequences of Choices .......................................................... 41
    Biblical Wisdom ............................................................................ 42
    Christian Entrepreneur Profile—William Colgate ......................... 43
    Executive Summary ..................................................................... 45
**Chapter Five—Biblically Based Business Goals**
    Long Term Goals ......................................................................... 46
    Short Term Goals ......................................................................... 49

    Handling Money ............................................................................ 49
    Wise Decisions ............................................................................. 51
    Christian Entrepreneur Profile—Dave Ramsey ........................... 52
    Executive Summary ..................................................................... 53

**Chapter Six—The Business Idea**
    Knowing What to Do ..................................................................... 54
    Choosing Your Business Idea ...................................................... 55
    Types of Income ........................................................................... 56
    Producers and Moochers ............................................................. 57
    Negative Impacts .......................................................................... 57
    Start Small at Home ..................................................................... 58
    Christian Entrepreneur Profile—Anthony T. Rossi ....................... 61
    Executive Business Summary ...................................................... 63

**Chapter Seven—The Business Plan**
    The Road Map to Success ........................................................... 64
    Outline of a Business Plan ........................................................... 65
    The Christian Entrepreneur Steps ................................................ 67
    Target Market Analysis ................................................................. 68
    Marketing Plan .............................................................................. 68
    Type of Business Structure .......................................................... 69
    Operations Plan ............................................................................ 71
    Christian Entrepreneur Profile—Tom Freiling .............................. 72
    Executive Summary ..................................................................... 73

**Chapter Eight—Reaching Out as a Christian Business**
    Our Purpose ................................................................................. 75
    Nine Jobs of a Christian Entrepreneur ......................................... 77
    Christian Entrepreneur Profile—Robert Norman Edmiston ......... 84
    Executive Summary ..................................................................... 85

**Afterword—The American Dream** ..................................................... 86

**Bible Study**
    Biblical Wisdom ............................................................................ 89
    Bible Study ................................................................................... 89
    Ambassadors of Christ ................................................................. 90
    The Blessed have a Mission ........................................................ 90
    A Giver's Heart ............................................................................. 91
    Building a Good Reputation ......................................................... 92
    Developing Your Staff .................................................................. 92
    Being Your Best ........................................................................... 92
    Staying Positive ............................................................................ 93
    Number One ................................................................................. 93
    Greatness ..................................................................................... 94
    Thinking Long Term ..................................................................... 94
    Finding a Niche ............................................................................ 95
    Standing Firm .............................................................................. 96
    Solid Business Practices .............................................................. 97
    Creating a Business Team ........................................................... 97

| | |
|---|---|
| Calculating Risks | 98 |
| The Golden Rule | 99 |
| Confrontation | 99 |
| Abundance | 99 |
| Accountability | 100 |
| Vision and Planning | 100 |
| The Rock | 102 |
| Accumulation | 102 |
| Tough Times | 103 |
| Fear and Anxiety | 104 |
| Mission Statement | 104 |
| Good Steward | 105 |
| Changing Your Heart | 105 |
| Meditate on the Word | 106 |
| Paying Your Bills | 106 |
| Charity | 107 |
| Spiritual Reward | 107 |
| The Importance of Knowledge | 108 |
| Make an Honest Profit | 109 |
| Rich get Richer, while Poor get Poorer | 109 |
| Humility | 110 |
| Innovation | 111 |
| Get Pumped! | 111 |
| The Bondage of Borrowing | 112 |

## Introduction
# God's Business Wisdom

After starting several businesses with varying degrees of success, the good Lord taught me that He had written in His Word the ultimate instruction manual to starting and running a business. I only wish a book like this existed when I was twenty-one years old and starting my first business. What absolutely blew me away was how Bible verses inspired by the Holy Spirit totally applied to today's business world. Truth is truth, whether it is written centuries ago or today.

> John 8:31-32 says *"If you keep my commandments, then you truly are disciples of mine. You shall know the truth, and the truth will set you free."*

I thought I was an expert on the subject of starting a business and getting off to a strong start in the rough and tumble business world. How wrong I was. It was disheartening to realize that almost all of the work I had done in the past would eventually turn to ashes. Worldly methods of starting and running businesses result in businesses that do not have an eternal impact. Normal businesses do not store up treasures in heaven and simply turn to dust.

Even if you have already started and own a business, you can convert it to an enlightened business using the Biblical principles in this book. God is totally forgiving of any past mistakes as long as you repent and turn toward His ways of doing business. You can make a fresh start today and be blessed mightily for it.

It is my prayer that you hear the voice of God in this book, not my own. Unlike a Donald Trump business book, I am not here to toot my own horn. The Lord is the ultimate business person and He wants to teach you how to be the ultimate you. Owning a Christ-centered business allows God to flow through every aspect of your business. Whatever knowledge that is His is also your knowledge. By allowing the Holy Spirit to guide your business decisions every day, you receive heavenly blessings that normal businesses can not even touch. God can be your greatest competitive edge in business.

Millions of people have come to the shores of the United States of America to pursue the American Dream. Hard work and wise investments can lead to owning your own business and earning a beautiful home and a better life for you and your family. All most people want is the freedom to try and live the American Dream.

Today excessive government regulation, the highest business taxes in the world, and enormous government and consumer debt threaten our freedoms. America is on the brink of disaster and the only thing that will save our economy and our country is to team up with God and start an avalanche of new Christ-centered businesses. It is up to entrepreneurs in the private sector to employ our workers again. Government is not the solution, it is the problem. This book will teach you how to pursue the American Dream through Christ.

By earning an honest profit and building wealth over the long term you can have a very positive impact on the lives of those around you and your community. As your business grows you can even have a positive spiritual impact on the entire country. America needs 1,000,000 more citizens to become millionaires in the next five years to put our economy back on track. Through Christ we can meet this challenge.

Is it moral to pursue wealth? Absolutely, how else can we turn our economy around? People are hurting because they do not have jobs. People are losing their homes because an unemployment check does not make ends meet. Dependence on the government does not work. It never has and never will work. Only by depending on God and learning from His wisdom can you build real long lasting wealth. I have never seen a poor man hire anyone. If you do not have a surplus of wealth how can you help anyone other than temporarily? You can give a man a fish or you can teach him how to fish. If you are wise, you will teach him how to fish.

There are many examples of faith-based businesses for you to model such as Tropicana, Colgate, Lord & Taylor, and Chick-fil-A. Whatever type of business you want to start, God is ready to be your business partner. Do not live a life of regrets—start living God's purpose for your life today. Start a business with the Lord today. Start an enlightened business.

> Luke 1:33 *"And of His kingdom there will be no end."*

Throughout this book I will place an executive summary at the end of each chapter. This will allow those in a hurry to get the basic information quickly and also allow easy review to prompt your memory. It is my recommendation that you review the Bible verses as well. So here is the first summary:

> **Executive Summary**
>
> 1. God has much to say about starting and running a business in His Word.
> 2. The Holy Spirit will guide your business decisions.
> 3. You can convert most existing businesses to an enlightened business.
> 4. God wants you to become the ultimate you.
> 5. Normal businesses do not have an eternal impact.
> 6. This book/seminar is about God and you—not me.
> 7. Earn an honest profit and build lasting wealth using God's principals.
> 8. It is moral to pursue the American Dream through Christ.
> 9. Only wealthy business owners can hire people.
> 10. Wealthy Christians are needed to help individuals, communities and our nation.

Chapter One

# The Christ-Centered Business

## The Enlightened Business

Is the Lord leading you to start your own business? If you have felt a spiritual tug in that direction, I have some good news for you. God wants to be your business partner! Most people already dream of starting their own business one day. So why not start your business with and for God? God will back you 100% if you start an enlightened business. Doesn't that make you feel much more comfortable and confident about your potential business venture?

Perhaps you have been laid off your job or you are looking for a home-based business that will allow you to spend more time with your family. There is no longer any job security in working for someone else. Loyalty is no longer rewarded in the work place. Pay rates are not keeping up with inflation as your family's real dollar income continues to shrink along with the declining value of the U.S. dollar. Owning your own business could mean job and financial security for you and your loved ones. By being your own boss you can create your own positive workplace atmosphere—a Godly workplace environment.

People start businesses every day, but most of them are not Christ-centered businesses. So just what is a faith-based business? A faith-based business is one that recognizes a higher power from day one. It is a Christ-centered business built upon biblical principles to glorify God while making a profit. In other words it is a business that realizes all things flow from God.

Since all things flow from God, ten percent of the gross profits from an enlightened business go to the Kingdom of God here on earth. A Christ-centered business tithes ten percent of its gross income to Christian causes from day one of being in business. This is important today more than ever since we are experiencing a difficult time economically around the world.

There is more to being an enlightened business than just acknowledging God's existence and tithing to His Kingdom. A faith-based business use biblical principles to design the business system and to formulate company policies. An enlightened company mirrors Christ and always asks the question—*what would Jesus do?*

Something else that may become more important if our nation's economy and the overall global economic decline continue is providing employment opportunities for Christians. Employment may also become an issue as the persecution of Christians around the world becomes more and more prevalent. Christian businesses can take care of the larger Christian family in tough times.

A Christ-centered business is run using the following basic principles that work in good economic times as well as bad;

1. Keep debt low
2. Keep reserves of cash

3. Create a written business plan
4. Write a marketing plan
5. Create fallback plans for tough times
6. Start each work day by meditating on the word of God
7. Make decisions after praying for guidance
8. Tithe ten percent of the gross profits to vetted Christian causes
9. Treat your employees as you would wish to be treated
10. Be involved in your community in order to help others

## God's Will for Your Life

God has a plan for your life and it is much bigger than you ever dreamed. You may also be surprised by what He eventually asks you to do. Because God wants you to become the ultimate you, He will challenge you. He may ask you to do something that you think you can't possibly accomplish. Alone you may not be able to bring about God's will for your life, but He asks you to lean on Him and use His strength. With God you can accomplish anything.

Initially His demands may not even make sense to you, but believe me, you need to listen and be obedient. If you do you will be blessed. If you do not, God will get your attention somehow, which is not necessarily fun.

So how do you recognize God's voice? Read God's Word every morning and keep it close to your heart every day. Pray often daily and ask for His guidance throughout the day. Memorize one verse of scripture per week for life. When you accepted Christ into your heart and became a Christian, He sent the Holy Spirit to dwell within you. The Holy Spirit acts like your conscience when it comes to making decisions.

## Enlightened Business Verses Greed

Many people in this country are pushing the idea that Capitalism is greed. Capitalism as an economic system is in need of a good public relations firm. In truth Capitalism simply describes the way we create an economic engine. The best new business ideas are considered by investors who vote with their dollars as to which idea they are going to support. By having a capitalization system based on investing in public offerings of stocks, we enable new businesses to raise money to start their businesses. Money, in particular cash flow, is the life blood of business.

The pursuit of money in and of itself is not greedy — it is taking care of your family and community. When you look out for your own best interests in a free market economy, you are placing yourself in the most effective place in our economy to make the best return on the investment of your time. By being efficient and productive in business, you are helping to lift the standard of living for all Americans.

Have you ever seen a poor man hire anyone? Only capitalized businesses and wealthy individuals can hire someone. Government can hire people as well, but only after taxing businesses and individuals. Governments do not create wealth, only businesses and individual workers create wealth. For each one million dollars in wealth that is created by an entrepreneur, it is used through our capitalistic engine to create ten new full time jobs as the economy expands! Jobs feed families, build communities, feed the poor, help the sick, and provide us with a positive purpose. Leave the lies that stir up class warfare behind and let's get real about making a difference in America! The truth is we need more millionaires in our country to help fix the mess our oversized government has gotten us into recently.

So what does God think of greed? He tells us in the Ten Commandments to not put any idols before Him. Money should never take the place of God as the most important thing in our lives. As Christians our priorities should be as follows;

1. Following God
2. Health
3. Family
4. The Christian community
5. Work and making money or formal education

Money is a tool that God uses to accomplish His goals for His earthly Kingdom. Money, like a hammer, is just a tool. It in itself is not good or evil. A hammer can be used to build a home for a family, or it can be used as a weapon to kill. Money is used for good and for evil purposes by people exercising the free will God gave them. The Bible teaches us to be good stewards of money, so that by using money properly, we can be blessed.

That public relations firm should be pointing out that Capitalism has pulled more people out of poverty and created more wealth than any other system in the history of the world. So if you want to really help the poor, start an enlightened business in a Capitalist economy. Is Capitalism perfect? No, nothing created by man is perfect. That is why we try to wisely regulate Capitalism to prevent any possible abuses such as monopolies. Sometimes the regulatory system fails and an Enron size failure occurs, or a Bernie Madoff type con-artist scheme slips through. Even with these problems and the pain they cause, a Capitalist economy beats a Socialist, Fascist, or Communist economy every time. History has proven it. If you do not learn from history you will repeat the same mistakes.

Even the godless Chinese Communists have figured out that Capitalism is the greatest economic engine in history. China is using Capitalism today to bring its country to the economic forefront of the global economy. So far Capitalism has lifted 400 million Chinese out of poverty and even created a new class of business millionaires and billionaires. As of this writing China has quietly become the second largest economy in the world, surpassing Japan and challenging the faltering U.S. economy that remains number one for now.

## Figure 1. The Business Environment
## Outside Influences on a Normal Business

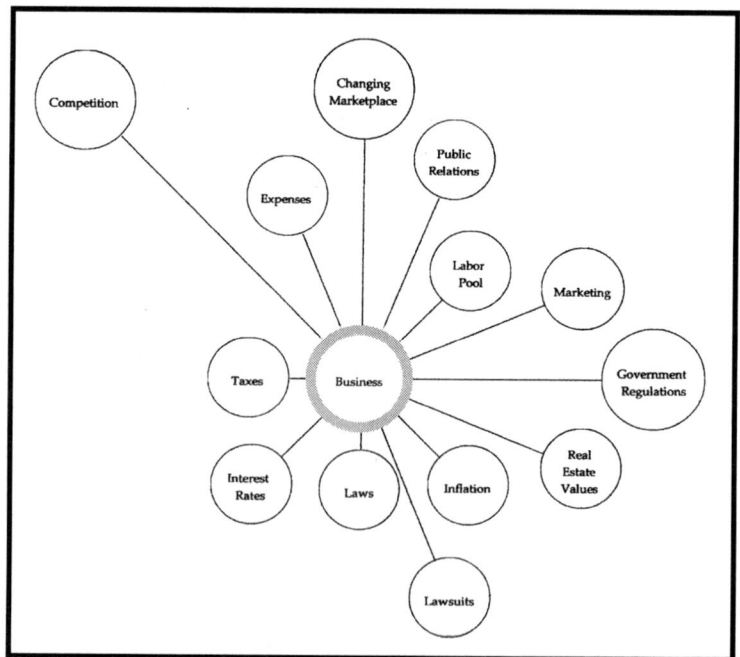

The world population exceeds 6.4 billion today. The U.S. population is a little more than 305 million. If you were to add up all of the charitable giving of other nations and put it up against just the United States of America, you would see that we donate more money than the rest of the world combined! Looking out for your own self-interests generates a surplus of wealth which we then share with the needy here at home and around the world.

Starting a Christ-centered business is a great way to take care of this public relations problem that most businesses seem to suffer from these days. On day one of business you announce in your Grand Opening press release that ten percent of the gross profits will be given to charities. This immediately makes you a company that is not based on greed, but on helping others.

Remember that an enlightened business is Christ-centered. That phrase means that Jesus is at the core of your entire business and its practices. Your business is a shining light in a world of darkness. Let the Holy Spirit flow through your business and you will be blessed and be allowed to bless others as well.

## Converting an Existing Business

Even if you have already started or purchased a business, you can convert it to an enlightened business using these same biblical principles. It is never too late to learn new and better methods of doing business. Rededicating your business to the Lord and changing your business practices to His way of conducting a business is an option you can believe is the right thing to do. God wants to work with you in your business to make your company, employees, and community a better place.

## Portable

> Revelation 16:15 says, *"Behold, I am coming like a thief. Blessed is the one who stays awake and keeps his garments, lest he walk about naked and men see his shame."*

As the Lord advises us, it is always good to be ready for the anything. Since we do not know what the future holds, it is wise to design a faith-based business that is portable. In the future it may be necessary to pick up and leave the U.S.A. in order to protect your family and employees from religious persecution and excessive government intrusion into the private sector of the economy. Over regulation by overly zealous bu-

### Figure 2. Christian Business Environment
### Additional Influences on a Christian Business

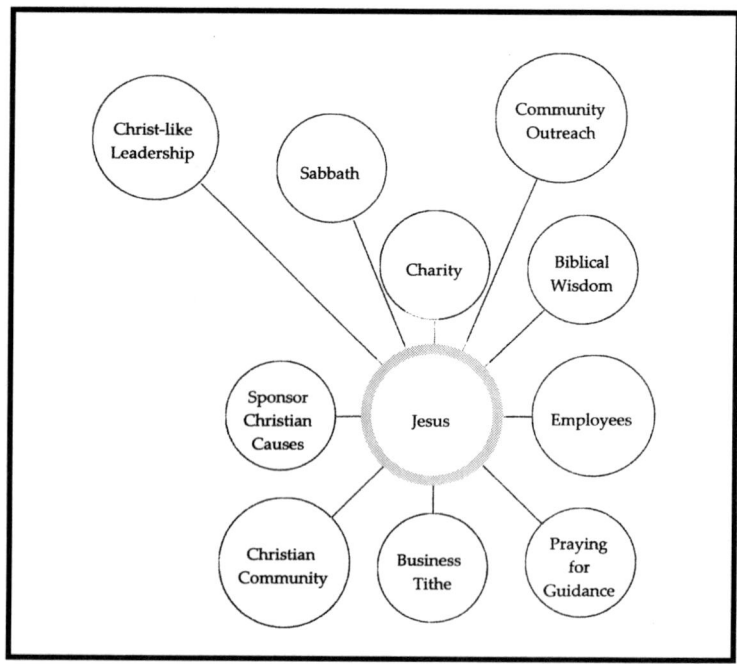

reaucrats in Washington can cripple a Capitalist economy. A change from Capitalism to Socialism or even an American version of Fascism would also destroy economic opportunity in this country.

A great example from history is our Jewish friends. For their entire history, Jews have been persecuted. Their collective response has been to value education that is portable and to own businesses that are mobile. The banking industry, the jewelry industry, international law, international trade, import and export businesses, or a wholesale business that sells to other businesses can all be moved to another more friendly country if needed. Internet based businesses and knowledge based businesses such as accounting and medicine can also be moved easily.

Nobody knows the future and I am not trying to predict it in this book, but Christians must always be on guard against those who have chosen to become our enemies. Today we Christians have many enemies within our own nation and threats from abroad that have reached our own shores through terrorism. Think religious persecution cannot happen here—that is what the Jews in Europe thought before World War Two. Be wise and be ready.

## A Call to Action

Since God the Father sacrificed His only Son Jesus to pay for our sins on the cross, He has chosen to work through His children—you and me. Yes amazing miracles still happen every day all over the world, but God relies on His children to stand up and say "I will." Starting your own enlightened business and partnering with God is standing up as a Christian leader. It is declaring that you are ready to make a difference in your community and in your country.

> Jeremiah 29:11 says, *"For I know the thoughts that I think towards you, says the Lord, thoughts of peace and not of evil, to give you a future and a hope."*

The bottom line is the best way for you to help your family and your greater Christian community is to start

---

## Executive Summary

**Reasons to Start a Christ-Centered Business**
1. Start a business that will have an eternal impact
2. Convert an existing business to an enlightened business
3. Allow God to help you become the ultimate you
4. Allow God to flow through every aspect of your business
5. Prayerfully allow God's wisdom to guide your decisions
6. Be obedient to God's will, so that you may be blessed
7. Allow God to give you a supernatural edge in business
8. Greater job security in rough economic times
9. With the Lord, create a Godly and positive workplace environment
10. To find a deeply satisfying work experience
11. Positively impact employees and their families' lives and the community
12. Sponsor children's sports teams, organizations, and schools

**A Christian's Priorities**
1. Following God
2. Health
3. Family
4. The Christian Community
5. Work and Making Money or Formal Education

*The Christ-Centered Business* 23

a Christ-centered business with God. An enlightened business stores up treasure for you in heaven. The rest of this book is about how to become an enlightened entrepreneur and how to incorporate biblical principles into the design and policies of your new Christ-centered business.

**Characteristics of an Enlightened Business**
1. Acknowledge a higher power—Christ the Son, God the Father and the Holy Spirit—the Holy Trinity
2. Tithe 10% of Gross Profits to churches or proven Christian causes
3. Understanding that all things flow from God
4. Use biblical teachings to design business systems and policies
5. Mirrors Christ
6. Helps Christian community and larger community
7. Do not work on the Sabbath
8. Keep debt low
9. Maintain six months of cash reserves
10. Start each day by meditating on the Word of God
11. Treat your employees as you would wish to be treated
12. Portable—you can move your business if needed

**Faith-Based Business Actions**
1. Pray for guidance from the Lord for all decisions (this will reduce stress)
2. Create a written business plan
3. Create a written marketing plan
4. Create a written backup plan (a fallback plan)
5. Tithe 10% of gross profits to vetted Christian causes
6. Be involved in your community—give time and sponsorships
7. Focus on doing one thing well and build a business around it.

## Chapter Two
# Leadership

**Preparing for Leadership**

When you decide to become an entrepreneur you are deciding to become a leader. It is important to prepare yourself for Biblically based leadership. There are ten choices you make to become a business leader and we will cover each of them.

In order to lead a business you must first humble yourself before the Lord. Realize that your strength and abilities alone you cannot succeed in business. You are not perfect, but God is perfect. God asks you to lean on His strength and wisdom by praying for His guidance before each business decision. Avoid becoming arrogant about your position in society and your success. Remember all things flow from God—including success.

Take responsibility for all parts of your life and do not blame others for failures. As a business leader you are ultimately responsible. You have probably heard the expression "the buck stops here". In business there can only be one boss for an employee to report to and that boss must manage all of the resources of the company and its employees well. By taking full responsibility you will earn the respect of your family, community, and employees.

The ability to truly forgive yourself and others is critical to your success in business. Holding in anger or negative thoughts will eat you alive. Releasing this pent up hostility is very important for your health and happiness. If you do not forgive those who have wronged you, you will block God's forgiveness of you and your sins. You literally cannot be a successful business leader without the ability to forgive.

The people you surround yourself with are important to your future success in business. Seek out good counselors who will give you Godly advice. Forget the image of the maverick lone wolf entrepreneur, in reality business is a team sport. You need great legal advice, great accounting, great tax law advice, great human resources advice, great marketing advice, great operations advice, great business strategy advice, great spiritual advice, etc. If your team isn't sharp, the competition will eat you for lunch!

Making good decisions is vital to managing a business. Before making any decisions, I recommend you pray to the Holy Spirit for guidance. Try to think of the effect of this decision on your business from all angles. How will this affect my customers? How will this affect my employees? How will this affect my business costs? How will this affect my community? How will this affect our profitability? Make decisions carefully and firmly and then stand by them. Being a great decision maker is a critical skill as a business leader.

In business it is best to drive your business plan forward and make things happen. Being pro-active and not reactive is much better for a business. It allows you to have an impact in the marketplace rather than reacting to changes in the marketplace. By being active in executing your business plan and marketing plan, you are shaping your business and gaining market share. Do not let your competitors define your business. You create the image and reality for your business.

Choose your attitude. You can choose to be a happy and positive person who exudes confidence. This is a very attractive personality trait of most natural leaders. You can choose to develop your positive attitude on a daily basis or you can choose to be inconsistent and moody. Which personality type would you want to follow?

Choose to be compassionate. Understanding and caring about the lives of other people is an important character trait of a leader. If you are wrapped up in your own life and never care to listen to others when they speak about their life, you will come across as cold, unemotional, and uncaring. Caring about your community and its well being will take your focus off of you and your problems and put things in the proper perspective while relieving stress. Life just seems to be better when you are thinking of others first.

Sir Winston Churchill was asked to give a commencement speech at a school graduation ceremony. The gritty British Prime Minister said, "Never, never, never, never, never, never, never…give up!" That was it. That was his whole speech! To reach your goals in life you must be persistent. There will always be challenges that attempt to get in the way of your dreams. It is how you handle those challenges and stay focused on the ultimate goal that will reveal if you are a winner.

A business or personal reputation is earned and very valuable. Protect your reputation by following through on commitments that you make. When you do what you say you will do, your reputation soars with those around you. You become an honorable and dependable part of the team. People want to do business with honorable business leaders. Keep your word when you give it.

## Nine Habits of an Enlightened Business Leader

1. Start your day reading the Bible. Immerse your mind in the Word of God and reinvigorate your thinking with the wisdom of our Creator. By reading the Word of God in the Bible, you are refreshing your memory with His voice and with His divine character. When you pray you can discern the voice of God better after reading His Word.

2. Pray throughout the day. As a child I was always taught to close my eyes when I prayed. This probably sounds silly, but one of the greatest lessons I ever learned as an adult was that you can pray anytime—even with your eyes open! You do not have to be in a church or on your knees nor have your eyes closed. You are free to talk to your God anytime and anyplace! My prayer time grew greatly when I was taught this simple lesson.

3. It is important to be an active listener. Do not let your mind drift when someone is communicating with you. When you are seeking an answer from God about a decision you have to make, be an active listener by focusing on God. Worship Him while you are waiting for an answer.

    *When I was taking Martial Arts for fun and exercise, the instructor had us meditate at the beginning of the class to focus our minds on what we were about to do. She would ask us to clear our minds. I would always picture Jesus in my mind during that meditation time. That would put my mind at peace and take it off my worries. Not a bad way to start something requiring a great deal of focus.*

4. Develop a daily action plan for your business. As you discern God's will for your business, it is important to map it out with a daily to do list. When the list is completed at the end of the day for the next work day, prioritize the actions steps. Make sure you get at least the five most important things done. Write a monthly set of goals, a quarterly set of goals and an annual set of goals designed to grow your business. It is okay if plans or goals change during the course of the year. Life is all about change.

5. Always strive to create a win/win business relationship. If you were to take advantage of someone in a business situation you would be breaking the golden rule. You deserve to make a profit in business, but not at the cost of your ethics and morals. A good reputation in business is earned, but one slip in your ethics can ruin your reputation and your business.

6. First gain an understanding of a business situation and then carefully try to be understood through clear communication. Only after you fully understand a situation can you communicate clearly. Do not jump the gun and make assumptions based on your own point of view alone. As said earlier, business is a team sport. Listen to your team or your customer first and then decide upon a course of action.

7. Bring together your wise counselors to creatively cooperate and find solutions for your business. A business leader is only as good as the information he or she receives. If you do not surround yourself with Godly and trustworthy people, you will get bad input from them and make poor decisions. Pray together for wisdom from God.

*Leadership*

8. Strike a careful balance between your personal life and your work life. Create time for your family on a regular basis. The family dinner table is very important to maintaining your relationships within your family. Workout together at the gym or at your home gym. Have a regular family prayer time. Take your spouse out on a date night at least once a month, so that you can be a couple without having to be parents.

9. Stimulate new thinking by reading or listening to books about your field of business and your faith. Keep growing spiritually and in wisdom over time. You will find that events occurring in unrelated fields may actually help you in your business. You have heard the expression "knowledge is power"? It is very true.

I was reading a news website the other day and found an article about the competition between five major corporations and how it would change the future of my business. Microsoft, Apple, Yahoo, Amazon and Google are innovating constantly in new technologies and services. What they are developing will completely change my multi-media publishing and seminar business in the next two years. If I had not kept up with business news, I would have been unable to anticipate and plan for the dynamic changes on the horizon. At least some of my competition would have been ready for the coming changes.

I am also an admitted seminar junkie. Learning new things is one of my favorite things to do. The Teaching Company offers *The Great Courses* on DVD, Audio CD's, or MP3 downloads. These are the very best college and university courses taught by the top professors. These courses are very stimulating and broaden your thinking.

## Executive Summary

**Ten Life Choices to Become a Business Leader**
1. The Humility Choice
2. The Responsible Choice
3. The Forgiveness Choice
4. The Counseled Choice
5. The Decisive Choice
6. The Active Choice
7. The Happy Choice
8. The Compassionate Choice
9. The Persistent Choice
10. The Honorable Choice

**Nine Habits of an Enlightened Business Leader**
1. Start your day reading the Bible
1. Pray throughout the day
2. Be an active listener to God and everyone
3. Develop a daily, monthly, quarterly, and annual action plan
4. Create win/win business relationships
5. Avoid making snap judgments, then communicate clearly
6. Bring together Godly and wise counselors as your business team
7. Balance your work and private life
8. Stimulate new thinking by continually learning

## Chapter Three
# The Art of the Start

**Start Here**

Square one on a board game usually says "Start Here". When you start a new enlightened business, the first thing you do is get on your knees and pray. Have you ever noticed from reading the Bible that Jesus did not teach his disciples how to preach? He did however teach them how to pray. So the first step in starting a Christ-centered business is to pray the following.

> *"Lord, help me discern Your will for my life and fulfill Your aspirations for me as Your child. Lord I sense the Holy Spirit is pulling me towards starting an enlightened business. Show me what business You would have me start and help me design it to glorify You in all ways and to serve Your purposes. In the name of Your precious Son Jesus I pray, amen."*

Why do you want to start a business? Most people answer that question by saying they want more freedom, more liberty, and more happiness than they can achieve working for someone else. You want a shot at achieving the American Dream!

Starting a faith-based business is the best way to pursue the American Dream. When you partner with God in business you get a supernatural edge to win in the competitive world of business. You win when you enable people to become their very best. You win when you serve others. You win when you share your blessings with others. You win when you become a fulfilled and happy entrepreneur. America loves a winner, so by joining with the ultimate winner according to the Bible and our Christian faith, you also become a winner.

## The Odds of Success

If you play the lottery (something I do not recommend) your odds of winning are printed on the back of the ticket. You have a 78 million to one chance of winning the Mega Million dollar prize. The chances of succeeding by starting your own business are one in ten. In other words one out of every ten businesses started in America are still in business five years later. Those are much better odds than wasting your money gambling. It is much wiser to invest in yourself by investing in your own business. It is even wiser to invest in a Christ-centered business which improves your odds of success that much more.

Even if you do not succeed the first time you start a business, by stepping out and starting your own enlightened business, you are learning valuable lessons. These lessons are better than a Harvard MBA degree, because they are gleaned from the real world, not the ivory towers of academia. You have heard the expression, "learn from your mistakes". In business this is critical to your long term success. Everyone makes mistakes, but if you pray about your decisions before you make the final decision, you will make fewer mistakes because you are leaning on the Lord's wisdom.

## Successful Businesses Defined

Have you ever read the issue of Forbes magazine when they profile the richest people in the world? Just focus on the top ten for a moment. Most of them do not have a college degree. Most of them had an inspiring idea for a business and acted on it. Most of them figured out a better system of doing something. All of them own their own business or multiple businesses. Quit making excuses about why you can't do it and have some faith in yourself and more importantly in God. He created you for a reason. Find out what that reason is and take action today!

There was a key phrase in the above paragraph. Someone figured out a better system of doing something. When you boil it down a business is a system of delivering a product or a service to a paying customer. When you create a successful system all you have to do is repeat the process again and again to make more money. When you hire an employee you teach them your system and duplicate yourself.

## Franchising

Some businesses naturally lend themselves to franchising. When you sell a franchise to someone, you train them how to duplicate your business system from top to bottom. The franchiser also acts as a continuing mentor to the franchisee(s) and helps them stay in business. In return you receive a monthly, bi-annual, or annual franchise fee for licensing your business system to another business person.

## Personal Financial Strength

God will answer your prayer about which business to start in His own time. Sometimes this is quite a while. The reason may be that you do not have your own financial act together enough to be able to start your own Christ-centered business. So after you have started your search for the right business idea, you also need to take

## Create a monthly budget

**Get a piece of paper, a pencil and a calculator out and write down the following monthly figures;**

- Take Home Pay
- Investment Income
- Other Sources of Income

*Add up these figures to determine your monthly net income (after tax income).*

**Leave a space and write down these monthly figures;**

- Tithe
- Mortgage/Rent
- Credit Card Payments
- Car Loan
- Health Insurance
- Life Insurance
- Auto Insurance
- Home Insurance

*Add up these figures to determine your monthly fixed expenses.*

**Leave a space and write down these monthly figures;**

- Heating
- Electricity
- Telephone
- Water and Sewer
- Groceries
- Automobile — Gas & Repairs
- Emergency Fund
- College Fund
- Retirement/401K/IRA
- Other Investments

*Add up these figures to determine your monthly flexible expenses.*

**Leave a space and write down these monthly figures;**

- Clothing
- Eating Out
- Personal Care (Haircut, Pedicure, etc.)
- Charity
- Vacation Fund
- Christmas/Birthdays Fund
- Other
- Recreation/Entertainment

*Add these figures up to determine your monthly discretionary spending.*

*The Art of the Start*

a good hard look at your personal financial success.

Strive to keep your focus on doing one thing well to earn income. By doing this you will become the master of that system of earning income. The Bible supports the concept of doing one thing well.

> Philippians 3:13-14 says, *"Brethren, I do not count myself to have apprehended; but one thing I do, forgetting those things which are behind and reaching forward to those things which are ahead, I press toward the goal for the prize of the upward call of God in Christ Jesus."*

### Create a monthly budget (cont'd)

At the top and to the right of these columns write the words, Budget, Actual, Difference. It is important to keep track of whether or not the difference is above or below your budget amount of spending. If you create a realistic budget you should be able to stick to it and with a little planning you will soon be on your way to a healthy financial picture.

Track your expenses on your Apple i-Phone, Blackberry, or purchase a small pocket notebook. List the above categories in your notebook and then record expenditures as you go. By writing down where your money is going, you will quickly begin to see where you are wasting money. Get serious about achieving your financial goals such as saving to start an enlightened business and you will find your backbone to tell yourself no when you need to do so. It is critical to reduce your debt as much as possible. This principle is true in your personal finances and in your business.

If it is necessary to reduce debt as quickly as possible you may need to create some additional income. Start with the smallest debt and pay it off first. Then move to the next smallest debt and keep going until you are free from the enslavement of debt. It will take time to get out of debt, but it will happen if you make a written plan to attack the problem.

Stay focused on God's will in your life. He has a plan for your life and that includes your business life. Always pray for His divine guidance whenever you have a financial decision to make. Keep it simple and repeat this humble practice in your personal, financial and business life. This system of making decisions with the Lord will greatly reduce stress in your life. God will direct you to the place of purpose He has for your life. Once there, you will discover God's power and receive His abundance in your life.

There are two ways to control your money. You can increase the amount coming into your life or you can decrease the amount going out. Sounds simple enough, but life happens and it is easy to get into debt and lose control of your finances. Debt is how to become enslaved and lose your personal freedom. To help you avoid the debt trap it is a good idea to create a monthly budget.

**Christian Entrepreneur Profile**

Chick-fil-A was founded as a single restaurant by Truett Cathy in Georgia. Truett grew his restaurant into a chain of over 1,400 locations without borrowing money from a bank. He also decided to close his restaurants on Sundays to give his employees a needed day of rest and to observe the Sabbath. Chick-fil-A offers a college fund for its employees and many of his employees that use that fund come back and continue working for the company. Chick-fil-A sponsors the SEC College Football Championship Game and a NCAA National College Football Bowl Game which is known as the Chick-fil-A Bowl Game.

Personally, Truett has helped literally thousands of Foster Children. He also taught a Sunday School class for decades at his local church, where he is a major contributor with his regular tithe. Truett was wise enough to start a Christ-centered business and follow God's will for his life. As a result he has made a huge difference in the communities his business touches and left a legacy of improved lives. I highly recommend you look up Mr. Cathy on the Internet to learn more about this very humble and very great man.

## Executive Summary

**The Art of the Start**
1. Pray for the Lord to guide you to the right business idea for you.
2. Gifts of the Spirit may be revealed to help you.
3. Reasons to start a business include more freedom and happiness.
4. By joining forces with the ultimate winner, God, you become a winner.
5. The odds of starting a successful business are one in ten.
6. If you fail, learn from your mistakes and try again.
7. A business is a system of delivering a product or a service to a paying customer.
8. Some business systems would make good franchises.
9. You do not need a college degree or years of experience to start a business.

**Personal Financial Strength**
1. Focus on doing one thing very well to create income.
2. Stay focused on God's will in your life.
3. You can control how much money you spend.
4. You can control how much money you make.
5. Create a written budget to get your finances under control.
6. Track your spending on your Apple i-Phone, Blackberry, or in a small notebook.

**Christian Entrepreneur Profile**
- *Truett Cathy, founder of Chick-fil-A*
  Look Mr. Cathy up on the Internet to see his amazing success story!

Chapter Four
# Biblical Teachings About Money

**Choosing the Wealth Path**

There are lessons in the Bible that will teach you how to gain financial freedom through supernatural means. This foundational wisdom can cause your business to succeed. These principles can take your personal finances to levels of abundance that you can scarcely imagine. To me Christians seem to be confused about money and how to create wealth and eventually achieve financial freedom. If this describes you, this chapter is very important for you to study.

More marriages end over money problems than for any other reason. What is bizarre is that financial failure cannot happen without your making decisions that create poverty in your life. On the other hand, creating wealth is a matter of studying what God's Word has to say about money and then following that wisdom like a road map to a hidden treasure. Your daily decisions about money will lead you down a path to poverty or to wealth. You have the free will to decide which way to go.

**Poor Money Decisions**

Poor decisions that will lead to poverty in your personal finances or your business finances include;

> Proverbs 22:7 says, *"The rich rule over the poor. And the borrower is the servant to the lender."*

Now this verse is not about class warfare or any other politically correct idea about bashing the rich in our country. (Remember, what we need is more millionaires to solve our nation's problems.) It is a statement of fact. When you decide to borrow money to purchase anything, you are creating a debt that you owe to another. For example, if you purchase a new car stereo system on a credit card, but you cannot pay it off when the credit card statement arrives you are making a decision that will make you poor.

> Proverbs 17:18 says, *"A man devoid of understanding shakes hands in a pledge, and becomes surety for his friend."*

Never co-sign or give a personal guarantee on a loan for someone else. Do not even consider it because if the other person does not pay, you are responsible for repaying the full amount of the loan plus interest. Avoid risking your good name for the sake of giving someone else credit.

> Malachi 3:9 says, *"You are cursed with a curse, for you have robbed Me, even this whole nation."*

You elect to be poor when you do not give God what is His. God has commanded that ten percent of your gross income (not your net income) should be given to His Kingdom here on earth. Make sure you are giving to a legitimate Christian cause or church that will use the money wisely as God wishes. Never steal God's tithe and always pay it first before any other bill.

> Zechariah 5:3 says, *"Then he said to me. This is the curse that goes out over the face of the*

> *whole land; for everyone who steals shall be cut off..."*

The above Bible verse sounds similar to the one before it, but this one is teaching you to not steal time or resources from your neighbor or your employer. God literally cuts you off from the flow of His abundance when you steal. He judges your thievery and punishes you for it supernaturally. It will seem like you never have enough money for your needs or wishes.

> Proverbs 13:4 says, *"The soul of a lazy man desires, and has nothing; but the soul of the diligent shall be made rich."*

If you are a freeloader who can work but chooses not to work, you are cursing yourself to poverty. In Jesus' day the average work week was sixty hours. By working only forty hours a week you are being lazy. Most millionaires work long hours in America. When you love what you do and you are making good money working why stop at forty hours a week?

David Foster is one of the most successful music producers and songwriters in the world. He works ten to twelve hours a day six days a week. He only rests one day a week. He says if he doesn't do that, a competitor will work that hard and eventually take his business away. I don't know if David Foster is a Christian or not, but he has learned one of God's lessons of creating wealth—maintaining a work ethic.

> Luke 15:12-13 says, *"And the younger of them said to his father, 'Father give me the portion of goods that falls to me'...the younger son... wasted his possessions with prodigal living."*

Wasteful living is a sin. Do you waste valuable things? Do you take for granted that you will always be able to buy more? God does not like a person who wastes possessions He has allowed to flow to you. This is another bad habit that will result in poverty.

> Genesis 12:3 says, *"I will bless those who bless you, and I will curse him who curses you; and in you all the families of the earth shall be blessed."*

God was talking about His chosen people—the Jews. If you are anti-Semitic or act against Jews in any way, you are cursing yourself to poverty. If you are wise and bless Jews with acts of kindness, you are choosing a path to prosperity. God can supernaturally bless you or curse you with ease, because all things flow from Him.

## Consequences of Choices

Money is not the root of all evil. It is just a tool to be used by people for good or evil. God provides you with money to be a good steward—in other words a good manager of these financial blessings. It is perfectly alright for you to enjoy material blessings as well. Not in a gaudy or show-off sort of way, but in a thankful way knowing that God is the source of those material blessings. God blessed David mightily.

> 2 Samuel 7:8 God says to David, *"I took you from the sheepfold, from following the sheep, to be ruler over My people, over Israel."*

Talk about a rags to riches story! David is a great example of a strong faith in God. We also saw David make poor choices such as his affair with Bathsheba. As a result of his poor choice David was punished by God. The universe that God created works the same way for you and me. It is like the law of gravity. If you make Godly choices you will be blessed. If you make sinful choices that alienate you from God you are cursing yourself and will suffer the consequences.

God blessed Solomon more than anyone else at that time with material wealth. If you were to calculate Solomon's wealth in today's dollars, my CPA says that would be more than $67 million annually.

> 1 Kings 10:14-15 says, *"The weight of gold that came to Solomon yearly was six hundred and sixty-six talents of gold, besides that from the traveling merchants, from the income of traders, from all the kings of Arabia, and from the governor of the country.*

If wealth and abundance is not a good thing, why would God bless His Son Jesus with it?

> Revelation 5:12 says, *"Worthy is the Lamb who was slain to receive power and riches and wisdom, and strength and honor and glory and blessing!"*

Your choices have consequences. Every single day you make choices with the money you are given to steward for God.

> Deuteronomy 30:19 says, *"I call heaven and earth as witness today against you, that I have set before you life and death, blessing and cursing; therefore choose life, that both you and your descendants may live."*

## Biblical Wisdom

> Proverbs 3:13-18 says, *"Happy is the man who finds wisdom, and the man who gains understanding; for her proceeds are better than the profits of silver, and her gain than fine gold. She is more precious than rubies, and all the things you may desire cannot compare with her. Length of days is in her right hand, in her left hand riches and honor. Her ways are ways of*

> *pleasantness, and all her paths are peace. She is a tree of life to those who take hold of her, and happy are all who retain her."*

That was Solomon telling you that wisdom is more valuable than silver, gold or rubies. Solomon asked God for wisdom and that wisdom produced great wealth! Wisdom, not wealth, brings you long life, honor, peace and happiness. The Bible is filled with truth. By studying the Bible you become wise. By following the wise teachings in the Bible it produces good judgment (choices) and leads you to wealth.

> Deuteronomy 29:29 says, *"The secret things belong to the Lord our God, but those things which are revealed belong to us and to our children forever, that we may do all the words of this law."*

God knows the secrets of wealth. When you pray to Him with a strong and unshakable faith, He will supernaturally bring you to the right place and the right time to receive blessings from Him. All kinds of blessings are His to give to you. Nothing is too hard for God. He can help your business become the ultimate enterprise well beyond your wildest dreams!

## Christian Entrepreneur Profile

William left home at the tender age of sixteen with all of his possessions stuffed into a bag that he carried in one hand. He wanted to find his place in the world, so he started looking for a job. In New York he met a man who was the captain of a canal-boat. William confided in the captain that his father was too poor to support him at home. He also told the captain that he only knew how to make soap and candles. The elderly captain's response was to kneel and pray for the boy.

When they again rose to their feet the captain told the young boy, "Someone will soon be the leading soap maker in New York. It can be you as well as someone else. Be a good man, give your heart to Christ, and pay the Lord all that belongs to Him."

The captain made quite an impression on William and he followed his advice. When he earned his first dollar, he gave ten cents to God. From that point on, he made it a habit to tithe ten cents of every dollar. He continued to be employed even through economically difficult times. Eventually, he became a partner in his employer's business and later he became the sole owner.

One-tenth of William's income went to the Lord and the business grew. As it grew William decided to give a larger portion of his income to the Lord. He gave twenty percent of his gross income, then thirty, forty, and fifty. His business grew and grew until William experienced an abundance of wealth. Finally he gave all of his income to God.

William chose to give his money to the Kingdom of God here on earth. He did not hoard the money, but rather let it flow from God through his Christ-centered business to him and then back to God. A great supernatural circle was formed and God blessed his business more and more. God honored William and I bet you know his last name—Colgate!

*Biblical Teachings About Money*

## Executive Summary

### Choosing the Wealth Path
1. The Bible will teach you how to manage money.
2. Most divorces occur over money issues.
3. Choosing to follow God's teachings can lead to wealth.
4. Your decisions are directly responsible for your financial situation.

### Poor Money Decisions
1. Borrowing money will keep you poor.
2. Never co-sign on a loan for anybody.
3. By choosing to not tithe to God you are stealing from God and cursing yourself to poverty.
4. Do not steal time or resources from your employer or neighbor.
5. Lazy people curse themselves to poverty.
6. Wasteful living is a sin.
7. If you are not the friend of the Jewish people (God's chosen people), you will be cursed by God.

### Consequences of Choices
1. Money is just a tool, not the root of all evil.
2. God wants you to learn to be a good steward (manager) of the money He entrusts to you.
3. Humbly enjoying material blessing is perfectly fine—do not brag or show off your wealth to make others envious.
4. God gave David, Solomon, and Jesus the blessings of wealth.
5. Your every day choices about money are important.
6. By following God's laws concerning money, you choose prosperity.

### Biblical Wisdom
1. Pray for wisdom
2. Wisdom is greater than wealth.
3. Wisdom produces long life, honor, peace, and happiness.
4. Great wisdom produces great wealth.
5. The Bible is the written source for our wisdom.

### Christian Entrepreneur Profile
- Use the Internet to look up the amazing life of William Colgate.

Chapter Five
# Biblically-Based Business Goals

**Long-Term Goals**

Now that you have prayed about what type of business to create, it is time to think about what you want to accomplish with that business. Planning for the future is wise. Setting short term, intermediate and long term goals help you decide where you want to go. Goals state where you want to take your business in a set time period. A business plan is a specific roadmap to success. We will talk about a business plan later in this book.

*What is the purpose of your business?*

1. **Glorify God**.

    1 Corinthians 10:31 says *"Whether, then, you eat or drink or whatever you do, do all to the glory of God."*

Reflecting the love of Christ the Son and the glory of God the Father by following the guidance of the Holy Spirit should be the purpose of your business. Do not hide your light as a Christian behind a corporate logo. Be a Christian first and a business leader second. Share the good news of the gospel with your employees, suppliers, vendors, customers, and community through your business. Pray before you act in order to make your actions something that will glorify God. Your goal is to build a Christ-centered business that God Himself can be proud of on a daily basis.

2. **Earn an honest profit.**

> Proverbs 11:24 says *"There is one who scatters, yet increases all the more, and there is one who withholds what is justly due, but it results only in want."*

Owners and employees of enlightened businesses should strive to maximize profits. Profits are the economic rewards for providing quality products and services to paying customers. Profits and more specifically cash flow are the life blood of a business. An unprofitable business will be forced to shut its doors and will be unable to accomplish any of the lofty goals it set out to achieve. A Christ-centered business cannot help anyone unless it first makes honest profits.

3. **Be a disciple of Christ and fund the teaching of the Gospel**

> 2 Timothy 2:2 says *"The things which you have heard from Me in the presence of many witnesses, these entrust to faithful men, who will be able to teach others also."*

It is important to share the Gospel with everyone around you. Your church, family, friends, neighbors, suppliers, vendors, distributors, employees and their families are the people that surround you. These are the people that you have the ability to impact in a positive way with the good news of Jesus Christ.

The best way to evangelize the people around you

is by mirroring Christ. By that I mean through your every day actions show that you do your best to be Christ-like. Of course you will fall short of the perfection of Jesus, but we as Christians are taught to die to self and allow Christ to live through us. Most people won't believe your words alone. People watch your actions and then decide to believe your words. This is how to truly influence people you come into contact with.

> James 1:22 says *"But prove yourselves doers of the word, and not merely hearers who delude themselves."*

A portion of your enlightened business should go toward the funding of those who spread the Word of God. The Holy Spirit will help you discern whether or not a person or organization is a good steward of the financial resources they are entrusted with by donors. Help spread the news of the gospel by helping to fund dedicated teachers, pastors or priests.

4. **Take care of your family and community.**

> 1 Timothy 5:8 says *"But if anyone does not provide for his own and especially for those of his household, he has denied the faith, and is worse than an unbeliever."*

Your family needs income in order to survive. An important function of your business is to take care of your family's physical needs. As your business grows you can also hire employees and help support their families as well. This is a great honor and responsibility that God may give to you through your service to Him. As your gross profits grow by following God's principles of building wealth, you can take care of more and more causes and people through your business. This cycle of the blessing of wealth then giving to charity leading to more blessings of wealth and to even greater charity is the result of following God's illogical rules to build wealth. The supernatural power of God creates the ever growing wealth cycle that creates the ever growing giving cycle. Just try to out give God—I dare you!

5. **Pay Your Bills**

> James 5:4 says *"Behold the pay of the laborers who mowed your fields and which has been withheld by you cries out against you and the outcry of those who did the harvesting has reached the ears of the Lord of Sabaoth."*

God will hold you accountable to pay your bills on time. This is part of being a responsible Christian business leader. Make your payroll obligations on time and pay your employees before you pay yourself.

## Short-Term Goals

After you have set long-term goals for your business, it is time to set short-term specific goals. Short-term goals are more operationally oriented for your Christian business. You must think about the short term goals of your specific type of business and write them down. When you have written goals to remind you of where you are going, you have a much better chance of success.

## Handling Money

In order to make a business operate well you have to set up a solid system for handling money.

1. Money priorities—cash flow is the most important thing to manage carefully.

2. Create a stable accounts receivable system to make sure that you are being paid by your customers on time.

3. Create a stable accounts payable system to make sure you are paying your bills on time to avoid any disruption of your business products or services to your customers.

4. Always tithe ten percent of the gross profits each month to a legitimate Christian church, ministry, or charity. This is your first money priority, because without it God cannot bless your business.

5. If necessary use an accounting professional to help you set up these cash flow systems on your company computer. Get these systems running correctly from day one to avoid problems in the future.

> Luke 16:13 says, *"No servant can serve two masters; for either he will hate the one, and love the other, or else he will hold to one, and despise the other. You cannot serve God and mammon."*

Your use of money will clearly show what you really believe. Our use of money is a good measurement of where we are in our spiritual lives. You can depend on the promises of God, but you cannot trust your feelings or reactions to the challenges of life. Choose to trust God first and foremost, even when circumstances look bad. In the long run you will see that you made a good decision by trusting the promises of God. If you are truly a disciple of Christ then it will show in your daily life.

> Mathew 25:40 says *"And the King will answer and say to them, 'Truly I say to you, to the extent that you did it to one of these*

> brothers of Mine, even the least of them, you did it to Me.'"

Treat your customers and employees well and always be honest in all of your business dealings. Your word as a Christian business leader is your bond.

> Proverbs 12:22 says *"Lying lips are an abomination to the Lord, but those who deal faithfully are His delight"*

So your financial short term goals are as follows;

1. Tithe to God
2. Pay suppliers and expenses
3. Pay employees
4. Pay taxes
5. Meet your own needs

> Philippians 2:3 says, *"Do nothing from selfishness or empty conceit, but with humility of mind let each of you regard one another as more important than himself"*

## Wise Decisions

Do not depend upon God to provide a miracle to save your business. There is a fine line between faith and the belief in miracles and testing the Lord. Do not test the Lord. Do not expect the Lord to bail you out if you make a poor business decision. Use your wise counselors and prayerful attitude to make good decisions. When you show obedience and a strong willingness to follow God's path, then He will bless you in His time.

> James 5:10-11 says, *"As an example, brethren, of suffering and patience, take the prophets who spoke in the name of the Lord. Behold, we count those blessed who endured…The Lord is full of compassion and is merciful."*

## Christian Entrepreneur Profile

Dave Ramsey was a real estate salesman and investor who had a financial net worth of $4 million when he was just 26 years old. His house of cards, based on too much debt, came tumbling down and Ramsey was forced to file for bankruptcy. Finally, out of pure frustration, he prayed to the Lord for wisdom about finances. He studied the Bible and found that God had a great deal to say about money.

At first Ramsey taught a Sunday school class about personal finances. In 1991 Ramsey and his wife founded Lampo Group Inc., a financial counseling business. At the core of his teaching was a slogan, "Act your wage!" In other words do not spend more money than you have and avoid debt. He also taught people to not become attached to material possessions and only pay cash for what you need. After becoming debt free it is okay to save up cash for what you want.

Today Dave Ramsey has written several national bestselling books including his signature book *Financial Peace University*. He reaches millions of people through his nationally syndicated radio show (*The Dave Ramsey Show*) and reaches 50 million more through his Fox Business Channel prime time cable TV show. Ramsey mixes business and his Christian faith every day in his teachings—to him it is a natural blending since he follows his faith through his business life as well as his personal life. Dave is far wealthier today now that he is following the Lord's way of handling money. Callers to his programs will ask him, "How are you doing?" The financial guru from Tennessee always answers, "Far better than I deserve!"

# Executive Summary

**Biblically Based Goals**
1. Goals state where you want to take your business in a set time period
2. Set short term, intermediate, and long term goals

**Christ-Centered Goals Include:**
1. Glorify God
2. Earn an honest profit
3. Be a disciple of Christ and fund the teaching of the gospel
4. Take care of your family and community
5. Pay your bills and taxes

**Money Handling Goals**
1. Manage cash flow effectively
2. Create an accounts receivable system
3. Create an accounts payable system
4. Tithe ten percent of your gross income to a church or charity
5. Use an accountant to set up money handling systems and pay taxes properly

**Short Term Financial Goals**
1. Tithe to God
2. Pay suppliers and expenses
3. Pay employees
4. Pay taxes
5. Meet your own needs

**Christian Entrepreneur Profile**
- Dave Ramsey the co-founder of Lampo Group Inc.

Chapter Six

# The Business Idea

**Knowing What to Do**

When you do not know what to do in any business situation what can you do? First you should pray to the Lord for answers.

> Jeremiah 33:3 says, *"Call to Me and I will answer you, and show you great and mighty things, which you do not know."*

Who has the answers? God. No matter what the situation, God has the solutions.

Second you study God's business guide—the Bible! His Words point the way to prosperity and success in business and life.

> Joshua 1:8 says, *"This book of the Law shall not depart from your mouth, but you shall meditate in it day and night, that you may observe to do according to all that is written in it. For then you will make your way prosperous, and then you will have good success."*

Third you write down your business idea, goals, and what will make your business unique verses the competition. Be diligent in executing your business plan. Plant the seed of your business in the kingdom of

God. The following Bible verse literally blew me away when I read it. The Bible, the Word of God, flat out tells you to write a business plan!

> Habakkuk 2:2-4 says, *"Then the Lord answered me and said: 'Write the vision and make it plain on tablets, that he may run who reads it. For the vision is yet for the appointed time; it hastens toward the goal, and it will not fail. Though it tarries, wait for it, for it will certainly come, it will not delay.'"*

## Choosing Your Business Idea

Select a business that you have a passion about. What type of business fascinates you? Remember you are going to be putting in long hours at times to get the business started, so it needs to be something that really interests you. Also answer the following questions;

What skills do you have that you can use in a business?

How much money do you have to invest?

Do you want or need investors to start your business?

What is the amount of return on investment you are seeking?

Are you willing to work longer hours and work harder than others?

Is your business idea a retail business, service business, manufacturing, import/export, educational, entertainment, restaurant or food service, consulting or professional (Medical Doctor, Lawyer, Dentist, or Chiropractor), or some other type of business?

What makes your business different? In other words, what is your Unique Selling Advantage?

A business is really a system for satisfying a need and cost effectively delivering that product or service to paying customers. Systems can be taught to employees down the road, who can eventually handle the running of your business while you oversee the operations as the owner or majority stock holder. What is your unique system of doing business?

## Types of Income

In 1984 a friend of mine founded a real estate investment firm while he worked full-time as a real estate agent. Today Coldwell Banker manages his investment properties. Eventually, he started a second business, a real estate finance business that invests in financial instruments such as discounted mortgages and tax lien certificates. It runs almost completely on automatic pilot. Later in 1996 he founded a book publishing company that grew into a multi-media publishing company and spun off a seminar company.

All of these businesses create passive income instead of active income. Active income means you get up and go to work to earn a paycheck. Passive income is being created whether you get up to go to work or not. He still gets up and goes to work, but now he does it because he is working on things that interest him. Design your business to eventually create passive income for you.

Each of my own businesses took long hours and hard work to get started, but eventually evolved from being active businesses to passive businesses. I can play with my wife and kids all weekend and still make money from my multiple streams of income as the businesses run on automatic pilot. The long term goal is to not have to work hard, but work because you love what you are doing. When you love what you do it doesn't feel like work. That is why retirement makes no sense to me unless you have lost your health.

## Producers and Moochers

Before Franklin D. Roosevelt's New Deal set a retirement age at sixty-five, no one retired unless they could no longer work due to poor health. Americans have always had a work ethic until the welfare state was set up. Then the government created a class of moochers. There are producers and there are moochers in this country today. Decide today to be a producer, not a moocher.

Once you have started a business it seems easier to start another. Many producers become serial entrepreneurs and found several businesses. Usually the businesses are in the same field or a closely related field than their first one. Sometimes it is a complete departure from the founder's zone of comfort. Pursuing a new challenge with a fresh idea is very rewarding to producers.

Entrepreneurs are risk takers, but they should not be stupid risk takers. You have all heard the cliché, "if you don't plan, you are planning to fail". Entrepreneurs use business plans and marketing plans to reduce the risks involved in starting and running a business. The love of taking on the challenge of building a business is what motivates most entrepreneurs.

### Negative Impacts

There are downturns to starting a new business. They include the following;

- Your income may suffer at first.
- Your work hours will become longer since you will be wearing many hats.
- Your family relationships and friendships may become strained.
- You may have spent your money reserves and may even be in some debt.
- You may become irritable and feel very tired.

*continued*

- You may sometimes feel like you are running behind and feel stress.
- You may get more headaches, stomachaches, or backaches and feel pressured.
- At first your life will seem like all work and no play.
- You may feel guilty when you are not working.
- You may forget to exercise and take care of your health.

These things are pretty normal when you start a business. Lean on the Lord's strength rather than your own. When you do, you can overcome obstacles and struggles that will inevitably occur in the process of creating a new business.

> Isaiah 58:11 says, *"And the Lord will continually guide you, and satisfy your desire in scorched places, and give strength to your bones, and you will be like a watered garden, and like a spring of water whose waters do not fail."*

## Start Small at Home

To reduce financial and mental stress, start small and build your business up from there. If you can hold down a full-time job and start your business part-time you can still earn a regular paycheck while you gain experience. When you have proven that your business system is a money maker, you can reverse the situation and work part-time for someone else. This method will also work to attract investors to your business, because it will have achieved a proven track record.

Starting small and building a business up also fits the biblical principle of not becoming burdened with debt. The point of starting your own business is to not work for others. When you borrow money, you are in fact working for the bankers. Some types of businesses require a business loan, but that needs to be thought through very carefully. Never personally co-sign or personally guarantee a business loan. Use other people's money in the name of a corporation as a separate legal entity or do not do it at all. If the business fails and you are personally responsible for the loan, you can destroy your family's wealth for a lifetime.

If you can start your business from home and avoid renting or purchasing office or warehouse space, you should definitely take this course of action. Do not automatically go out and purchase a brand new computer, printer, or a desk and chair unless you need them. My home office is an 8' by 10' sitting room off the Master Bedroom in my house. I use an old scratched up rosewood dining room table as my desk and a comfortable executive style chair that rolls around. I have a used filing cabinet, cheap wooden bookcase, and an old scratched up end table in the room for my radio/CD Player. I have three computers which are all laptops and two printers that are also copy machines and scanners.

When I am at my home-office, I use one computer for the Internet and email and one computer for writing at the same time. If I am in my car I have a power converter that allows me to plug a laptop into my car. My family of five has one cell phone each and I use an Apple i-Touch for mobile Wi-Fi connections to the Internet and email. I prefer a separate cell phone/camera and an Apple i-Touch so that I can comfortably speak on the phone while surfing the Internet. Some people like the all-in-one features of an Apple i-Phone or an Apple i-Pad. Whatever your preference and depending upon your type of business, it is important to invest in the equipment you truly need to be the most efficient you can be. Keep it practical and do not get caught up in the gadget happy world of techies.

Working from home allows me to see more of my family and reduce stress by being in comfortable surroundings. Make sure to draw the lines with your family about business hours verses home life hours. Family members may have a tendency to not think of you as working when you work from a home office. Be firm about keeping work time for work and not errands or a honey-do list the length of your arm.

Practice focusing on your work. I wrote this chapter sitting in the Great Room while a TV was on and my wife was meeting with two other teachers for a Graduate School project ten feet away. My wife was amazed that the entire chapter only needed three corrections. I write about five hundred edited words an hour. This comes from years of practice writing fiction and nonfiction. What skills can you improve to make yourself more productive every day?

My father is a retired Radiologist who could read 1,500 words per minute while watching a big TV with two smaller TV's stacked on top. The TV's were tuned to CBS, ABC, and NBC at the same time. You could ask him a question about any of the TV programs or the book and he could tell you exactly what was going on. Now that is productivity while being entertained! You can train yourself to do all sorts of things you never dreamed possible.

The next step is the virtual office. This is when a receptionist answers your office line and you have access to a beautiful office or meeting space in a nice office building when you schedule it. Some clients need to see a professional office to feel good about working with you. If this is the case with your business, then by all means use a virtual office space to impress clients. A company I recommend is Regus Offices and they can be reached at 1-800-OFFICES by phone.

If your type of business needs a restaurant, offices with a warehouse attached, or several offices, use a commercial real estate agent to show you around. Be thorough and look for bargains before you commit your corporation to a lease or purchase. It is okay to start in humble surroundings in some businesses. Making a profit is the goal, not a rent payment on office space.

Finally a car or vehicle may be a necessary part of your business. I drive an American made mid-sized sedan that gets excellent gas mileage. It is nice looking and I keep it clean on the inside and out, but it is not an expensive car designed to impress. It is practical, which is the image I want to convey to my clients. Match your vehicle to your customer's expectations according to the industry that you are in, but go with a used vehicle in the first five years of the business and never personally co-sign for the business car loan. Try to buy a used vehicle for cash.

One more word about business cars is needed. If you run a business that has employees and you commute to the location every day, do not drive up in a Corvette or even a Mercedes. Employees resent business owners that are flashy with their cars. Sam Walton the founder of WalMart, drove an old American made pickup truck to work. While I am not saying this is necessary in all cases, be careful about the image you are creating through your choice in vehicles. You may want to consider getting a "wrapped" SUV that is literally a mobile billboard for your business. This is a practical method of advertising that is effective for many types of businesses.

## Christian Entrepreneur Profile

Anthony T. Rossi was an immigrant from Italy who founded Tropicana Products in 1947. The orange juice producer started in Bradenton, Florida with 50 employees and by 2004 grew to employ more than 8,000. Over the years Tropicana expanded into multiple product lines and became one of the world's largest marketers and producers of citrus juice.

In 1954, Rossi invented and patented a pasteurization process to aseptically pack pure chilled juice in glass bottles. This process allowed the juice to be shipped and stored without refrigeration. For the first time, it was possible to offer consumers the fresh taste of orange juice made from 100% fruit over a widespread area. Another breakthrough came shortly after when Rossi devised a method of freezing citrus juice in twenty gallon blocks for storage and shipping. He also was a pioneer who introduced citrus products into school food programs.

Rossi was known for being a religiously-oriented businessman who made annual pilgrimages back to his native Sicily. He helped build a church and mission in Sicily. In the United States he endowed the Aurora Foundation which funded various Christian programs and other charities.

In 1978, Rossi sold Tropicana Products to Beatrice Foods and retired. He continued to work through his Aurora Foundation to help Christian causes and charities until his death in 1993. Tropicana is now a division of PepsiCo and is the world's largest producer of branded fruit juices.

*The Business Idea* 63

## Executive Summary

### The Business Idea
1. Pray for answers to all your questions
2. God is the answer. God has the solutions.
3. Study God's business guide—the Bible
4. Write down your visions in a business plan
5. Select a business you are passionate about
6. Match your skills, hobbies, and interests with a business idea
7. Find a unique business system that will offer a unique selling advantage
8. Decide to be a producer, not a moocher

### Negative Impacts of Starting a Business
1. Low income at first
2. Long work hours
3. Possible strained relationships with family and friends
4. Having invested your money, you could be temporarily broke
5. Stress can cause physical ailments such as stomach aches, headaches, and backaches
6. You can become over-tired and irritable
7. May feel guilty when you are not working
8. May forget to exercise and maintain health (exercise helps fight stress)

### Be Conservative
1. If possible start a home-based business
2. Buy used furniture, filing cabinets, chairs, desks, and maybe even computers
3. Use cash whenever possible to avoid debt
4. Incorporate and offer stock if you need to borrow money to get started
5. Never personally guarantee a business loan (don't co-sign on a business loan)
6. Develop your computer skills, reading speed, and multi-tasking to improve your personal productivity.
7. Focus your brain and don't get distracted
8. Start with a used business vehicle that matches the needs of your business and image

### Christian Entrepreneur Profile
- Anthony T. Rossi, the founder of Tropicana Products.

Chapter Seven
# The Business Plan

## The Road Map to Success

Putting your business idea and plan into a word processing file is a crucial step and can at first seem very intimidating. For one thing many people do not like to write or feel they are not very good writers. What I always tell people is that no one is as passionate about your new business idea as you are so it is important to write your own rough draft. I am a professional writer, but when I write a rough draft I am literally typing as quickly as I can to get my ideas down on paper. I clean up the rough draft and make it readable later. You can always hire a professional writer out of the yellow pages to help you perfect a final draft.

Perhaps speaking about your idea works better for you—you can speak into a handheld MP3 recorder then hire a transcriptionist to write it all down. There are also software programs such as Talk It, Type It and Dragon Speak that allow you to talk into the built in microphone in your computer and the software will create the text for you in a word processing program. Do not hire a "Business Plan Writer" to write your plan for you, or at least not until you have written a first draft. You must communicate your passion for your

*The Business Plan* 65

business idea and then think about going to a writer to help you edit the flow and grammar of the plan.

Writing a business plan is a proven way to develop your business idea fully and it definitely contributes to a successful business start-up. The process of writing a business plan forces you to systematically think through your idea in detail. Another way to describe a business plan is to compare it with a blueprint that you follow to build something—in this case your piece of the American Dream.

Once written, a business plan can also be used to present the business to outside investors or bankers. Investment bankers, angel investors, venture capitalists, your rich Uncle…all need to see a business plan in order to decide whether or not to fund your idea. Planning out your business start-up will reduce the stress and anxiety that new entrepreneurs can experience. A strong business plan anticipates obstacles and provides solutions for overcoming them in order to get the business off the ground.

> **Outline of a Business Plan**
>
> Business plans can be from three pages to over one hundred pages in length, but the average is around thirty pages. Today's business investors look at between thirty to fifty business plans per day. In order to get through that many in one day, they only read the first part of the business plan in order to decide if the rest is worthy of their reading time.
>
> So the executive summary is the most important part of your business plan. To use an old cliché—you never get a second chance to make a great first impression.

> **A sample outline of a business plan follows;**
> I. Executive Summary
> II. Company Description
> III. Industry Analysis
> IV. Target Market Analysis
> V. Marketing Plan
> VI. Type of Business Structure, Key Personnel and Management Team
> VII. Operations Plan
> VIII. Details of Product or Service with a Development Plan
> IX. Profit and Financial Projections
> X. Appendix (Sources of your research)

A business plan has facts and figures revealed by your research, but it should also build anticipation to see the vision of a new venture move from concept to reality. It is important to create a business plan that excites potential investors, employees, and anyone potentially involved in the business about the idea. Your plan must sell the feasibility of the idea and the strengths of your key personnel *and management team*. Very often the quality of your management team will make or break your plan with the investors of today. New entrepreneurs can substitute experience with enthusiasm for a new business concept firmly based in a realistic understanding of the marketplace.

The key is to learn about the potential of your business through the process of writing a business plan. This will give you the confidence to move forward or help you make the decision to not pursue a particular business idea. Realizing that a particular business idea is not practical or feasible is disappointing, but it is much better to fail on paper than in the real world.

Remember nine out of ten new businesses fail in the first five years. A well researched business plan greatly increases the odds of success.

## The Christian Entrepreneur Steps

Remember you should not try to be a lone maverick when you are starting a business. Business is a team effort! Even if you have started several businesses each business idea is unique so good honest feedback is important. That is why I developed the Christian Entrepreneur Steps to make sure you have the best shot at success. If you follow these steps you will know what you are doing and how to go about turning your dream into reality. The Christian Entrepreneur Steps are:

Step One—realizing God's calling to start a business.

Step Two—attend The Christian Entrepreneur, Build a Christ-Centered Business seminar to learn Biblical-based wisdom about finances and business.

Step Three—write a rough draft of your business plan.

Step Four—bring your rough draft to The Christian Entrepreneur Boot Camp to get feedback from a small group of your peers about your business idea and plan.

Step Five—complete the final draft of your business plan and take it to a Small Business Development Center or SCORE (www.score.org) chapter in your area for a final critique.

Step Six—consider joining The Christian Entrepreneur Club for continuing information about building a Christ-centered business and to be among like-minded people.

Step Seven—Start your business!! Avoid analysis paralysis!

## Target Market Analysis

It has been my experience that this is one area where you may not understand exactly what to write about. A target market is the specific group of people you are offering a product or service to in the marketplace. In this part of your business plan you need to answer the following questions:

Who is your target market?

What is the age group of your target market?

Is there a specific geographical location where you can find them?

Does your target market belong to any associations or organizations that you can reach them through?

Do they attend trade shows or conventions of any kind?

What sort of media do they consume? (TV shows, radio shows, magazines, newspapers, newsletters, online magazines, Internet news groups, podcast shows, websites, music, Internet search engines, etc.)

What is the most effective way to reach them? (Print or broadcasting advertisements, networking, churches, Internet marketing, signs and billboards, bumper stickers, business cards, brochures, direct mail, flyers, sales force, multi-level marketing business, infomercial, word of mouth, professional reputation, writing a book, etc.)

## Marketing Plan

You do not need a college degree in marketing to write a marketing plan. A marketing plan explains what marketing materials you will need to create such as a brochure or a radio spot to reach your target market. Is your marketing going to start locally then go regionally then go national then go international? Outline your marketing budget and reveal how it will grow and change as your business develops. Be as specific as you can, but do not try to write a TV commercial and put it in your marketing plan. No one expects you to be a one person advertising agency.

## Type of Business Structure

What type of business are you going to start? There are roughly six different types of businesses that you can start:

1. Sole Proprietorship
2. Partnership
3. "S" Corporation
4. "C" Corporation
5. Non-Profit Organization
6. Limited Liability Company

The reason I say "roughly six different types" is that there are actually several different types of Limited Liability Companies that you can start depending upon which state you live in. You should always consult a Certified Public Accountant (CPA) and or a business attorney to determine which legal business entity is right for you and your business idea.

I will say emphatically—do not start a Partnership with anyone period! In a Partnership each partner gets a stake in the business no matter how hard they work, they all get the same amount of ownership. It can be two partners or ten partners, it doesn't matter. Owning your own business is about control and working hard for yourself—not your lazy partner. If you do create a partnership, agree upfront how you can dissolve it. All too often one partner becomes the true leader of the company and the other just rides his coat tails. Employees can only report to one boss, not ten different bosses at the same level in the business. A Partnership is a business divorce waiting to happen.

A sub-chapter "S", or simply known as an "S" Corporation, allows you to be taxed at your personal income tax rate on business earnings. It also allows a personal income tax rate on what the corporation actually pays you as income. In simpler terms—it helps you avoid double taxation of the money you earn from your business. Any income or deductions generated by the corporation passes through to the shareholders, who pay individual taxes on it. You become an employee shareholder of you "S" Corporation.

The "C" Corporation is expensive to form and expensive to maintain. You have to generate much more paperwork, hold more meetings pay for more accounting services, publish your company records, and pay more legal bills with this form of business. You are also double taxed—once at the corporate tax rate and once again on salaries, commissions, and bonuses paid to employees as income at their personal tax rates. "C" Corporations are usually large publically traded businesses like General Electric or Exxon. "C" Corporations are separate legal entities that can own anything a person can own such as cars, houses, boats, and office buildings. An advantage of this type of business is that you can sell stock to capitalize your business or to expand your business.

Probably the simplest form of business is the Sole Proprietorship. As a Sole Proprietorship, whatever the business earns is yours to keep. On the other hand, any debts incurred by the company are considered your personal debts. Literally you are the business and the earnings are taxed at your individual tax rate. This structure is great for small business. To protect your family's assets in case of a lawsuit, simply purchase an umbrella liability insurance policy attached to your home and auto insurance policies. Also I recommend becoming a client of Pre-Paid Legal Services to maintain a law office on an inexpensive retainer in case of potential legal problems. As the key person in this type of business you also need a term life insurance policy to benefit your family in case of your untimely death.

The next business structure is the Limited Liability Company (LLC) that helps to limit your personal liability. An LLC issue stock to the owners and is less expensive to form, less complex to manage, while offering far better tax treatment than a "C" Corporation. It can also provide many of the same benefits that a "C" Corporation can offer. This is a great second step for a small business as it grows past about $55,000 per year income. Today there are several different tax treatments that you can choose from as an LLC. Consult with your CPA to help you set up an LLC properly from the beginning.

Choosing to become a Non-Profit Organization instead of running a commercial business is sometimes a good idea. If your business idea is designed to raise money to help people in need directly, this is the right business structure to use. However, this is an expensive and time-consuming organization that is highly regulated by the government. You must be very careful to show how income is used after expenses to benefit others.

## Operations Plan

All commercial businesses can be boiled down to a system of providing a service or product to a paying customer. An operations plan can be a flow chart that shows how the product is manufactured, packaged, distributed, and sold to the target market. It can be a weekly or monthly work flow explanation. You can explain the steps involved in making your business work on a daily basis. The operations plan will vary widely since all businesses are unique, just like the individuals who start them.

**Christian Entrepreneur Profile**

Tom Freiling is a speaker, author, and serial entrepreneur. He is the former managing director of Eagle Publishing in Washington, D.C. and publisher of Creation House in Orlando, Florida which he founded with a group of Christian entrepreneurs. He is also the founder and publisher of Xulon Press and the author of several books. Freiling is the bestselling author of *George W. Bush on God and Country* (Allegiance Press), *Prayers to Move Your Mountains* (Thomas Nelson), *Abraham Lincoln's Daily Treasure* (Revell), and *Reagan's God and Country* (Gospel Light). He has sold more than two million books worldwide and appears on syndicated radio shows and on cable TV on channels such as CNN and C-Span among others. *Writer's Digest* magazine wrote a feature article on Freiling and named him one of the world's leading experts on self-publishing.

Currently, Freiling serves as founder and CEO of Samaritan Fundraising in Washington, D.C. Samaritan Fundraising is an innovative church and ministry fundraising company. The motto that Freiling lives by is "We make a living by what we get, but we make a life by what we give."

*The Business Plan*

## Executive Summary

**Business Plan**
1. Write down your business idea
2. Research you potential industry
3. Write down a business plan to fully develop your idea
4. You must convey your passion about your idea
5. You must write the first draft of your business plan
6. Write down a business plan for:
    A. Potential investors
    B. Bankers
    C. Potential employees
    D. Your Certified Public Accountant
    E. Your attorney
7. A business plan is a practical road map to success

**Elements of a Business Plan**
1. Executive Summary—the most important part
2. Company Description
3. Industry Analysis
4. Target Market Analysis
5. Marketing Plan
6. Type of Business Structure, Key Personnel, and Management Team
7. Operations PlanvDetails of Product or Service with a Development Plan
8. Profit and Financial Projections
9. Appendix (Sources of your Research)

**Christian Entrepreneur Steps**
1. Realizing God's calling to start a business
2. Attend The Christian Entrepreneur, Build a Christ-Centered Business seminar to learn Biblically-based wisdom about finances and business
3. Write a rough draft of your business plan
4. Bring rough draft to The Christian Entrepreneur Boot Camp—limited to ten people to get honest feedback and help from your peers

*continued*

5. Complete the final draft of your business plan and take it to local SCORE chapter for final feedback
6. Consider joining The Christian Entrepreneur Club for continuing information about building a Christ-centered business and the be among like-minded people
7. Start your business—avoid analysis paralysis!

**Target Market Analysis**
1. The specific group of people your product or service is designed to help is your target market.
2. Answer the who, what, where, when and why questions detailing the characteristics of your target market.
3. Answer the how question about how you are going to reach your target market

**Marketing Plan**
A marketing plan details a marketing budget and what specific marketing tools will be used to reach the target market.

**Type of Business Structure**
1. Sole Proprietorship
2. Partnership
3. "S" Corporation
4. "C" Corporation
5. Non-Profit Corporation
6. Limited Liability Company—there are several tax treatments and different structures within an LLC structure. Always consult a CPA or business attorney before choosing a business structure to avoid potential problems down the road.

**Operations Plan**
All businesses are essentially systems of providing a product or service to a paying customer. This part of the business plan answers the following question: What is the specific system will allow your business to operate on a daily, weekly, monthly and annual basis?

**Christian Entrepreneur Profile**
- Tom Freiling, serial entrepreneur.

Chapter Eight

# Reaching Out As a Christian Business

**Our Purpose**

Congratulations! You are one of a minority of people on this planet who has figured out the big picture. Through deep thinking you have discerned that Christianity is the one religion that offers forgiveness and redemption that no other religion can match. Using your free will you have sought out and started a personal relationship with Jesus Christ, whom you have selected to be your Lord and Savior. That is noteworthy and impressive in this modern world that is jammed with information and a hatred and bias against Christians.

In America today it seems everyone but Christians are afforded freedom of speech. Christians can't make fun of other religions, but it is very acceptable to mock Christianity. We are literally the butt of joke after joke in our own homeland. Now I love a good joke as much as the next guy, but when attacks on Christianity are disguised as humor that crosses the line.

Even our legal system is being used to attack Christians. Under the new "hate crime" legislation passed by our federal government, a pastor cannot teach a comparative religions class that shows why Christianity is the one true religion without opening himself up to prosecution in our legal system for "hate speech".

Every day more and more of our religious freedom is being eroded by the American Civil Liberties Union (ACLU) and secular humanistic beliefs in our society backed by new laws and cultural beliefs.

Non-Christians look at Christians and say we are;
1. Narrow minded
2. Judgmental
3. Anti-science (being ignorant or uneducated)
4. Prejudiced against homosexuals
5. Prejudiced against other religions (intolerant)
6. Trying to force others to conform to our set of beliefs
7. And the most popular—Christians are a bunch of hypocritical jerks.

These are "Hot-Button" issues that can inflame people and start huge arguments within families, communities, and even churches. Clearly people have forgotten that the U.S.A was founded on Christian beliefs and values. On the one hand, Christians are taught to love our neighbors and our enemies, but on the other hand, we have to defend our freedom of religion and our faith. We are told to embrace people and bring them into the church, but we need to be discerning as to who we can trust or should associate with in our lives. Our nation's laws order us to not discriminate based upon religion in the hiring process, but we want to run a Christ-centered business. These are tough issues that Christians and Christian entrepreneurs face on a daily basis.

As Christians in business we have to walk a fine line. Striking a balance between faith and living and working in the real world is not easy. Remember our entire purpose for remaining on earth after we have been saved is to shine a light of hope and love into a dark and fallen world. We are supposed to be spreading the good news of Jesus Christ to the four corners of the planet. So how do we reach out to the world as a Christian business?

> In Mathew 5:14-16 Jesus says *"You are the light of the world. A city set on a hill cannot be hidden. Not do men light a lamp and put it under the peck-measure, but on a lamp stand; and it gives light to all who are in the house. Let your light shine before men in such a way that they may see your good works and glorify your Father who is in heaven."*

## Nine Jobs of a Christian Entrepreneur

God has a purpose for each of us, but it is up to us to discern what that purpose is and to act upon that knowledge.

> Colossians 1:9-14 says, *"For this reason also, since the day we heard of it, we have not ceased to pray for you and to ask that you may be filled with the knowledge of His will in all spiritual wisdom and understanding, so that you may walk in a manner worthy of the Lord, to please Him in all respects, bearing fruit in every good work and increasing in the knowledge of God; strengthened with all power, according to His glorious might, for the attaining of all steadfastness and patience; joyously giving thanks to the Father, who has qualified us to share in the inheritance of the saints in light. For He delivered us from the domain of darkness, and transferred us to the kingdom of His beloved Son, in whom we have redemption, the forgiveness of sins."*

**Job one** is to walk the talk. Your actions speak much

louder than your words. Non-Christians will watch your actions very carefully, looking for a false move that will allow them to attack you. Each morning pray to the Lord and tell Him that you are His to use for His purposes that day. Study a Bible verse that relates to running a business and pray for God's wisdom and discernment every day. Help your neighbors and your community in the course of running your business. Put others first and make sure you do not harm anyone with the actions you take. Show love in your actions, even if sometimes it has to be tough love. Reflect Christ by letting go of your own ego and selfish tendencies (die unto yourself that Christ may live through you).

**Job number two** is to offer time for prayer and Bible study at the workplace before or after work hours, during break times and lunch time. If pagans see you praying and reading your Bible and seeking God's wisdom to help you run your business they will be attracted to Christianity. Be consistent in this area and make sure you invite everyone to participate.

**Job number three** is to openly support causes and charities in your community that reflect your Christian values. Be careful here to discern (yes judge) which causes and charities truly are working to better the lives of others in a way that matches our Christian beliefs. For example, The American Red Cross is an excellent charity that provides blood to hospitals, food, clothing and shelter to disaster areas and victims of fires. Many people think The American Red Cross is a Christian charity—it is not. However, The American Red Cross reflects the values of Christianity and is therefore worthy of support.

The International Red Cross is a semi-political group that hides behind a non-profit organizational mask. The political affiliation that it backs is Global Socialism which is highly anti-Christian, anti-capitalist and anti-democracy. The International Red Cross will lie outright to further the cause of Global Socialism and is not to be trusted.

Another organization that claims to be charitable, but is not worthy of Christian support is The United Way. It collects money which it then sends to other organizations that do the actual charitable work. Unfortunately, most of the money it collects goes to support its own expensive overhead costs. Very little money gets used to actually help people in need. The United Way also funnels money to Planned Parenthood which provides pro-abortion counseling and abortion services. Most people do not know that Planned Parenthood was started by a racist to abort the babies of minorities in America. This is another sick and twisted organization disguised as a group doing "good" for the community.

The bottom line is to be very careful about which charitable organizations you support. Research what percentage of monies collected actually goes to help others and how much goes to the organization itself. Pray, research, and discern before you give.

**Job number four** is to have a sense of humor about yourself and your faith. God has big shoulders and He can take a joke. After all He invented humor. You are not perfect which is why you need Jesus to pay for your sins. No matter how much we try not to, we are going to make mistakes. Do not take yourself too seriously. Admit when you make a mistake. Apologize and pray for forgiveness one time and mean it. Do not go on an apology tour or dwell on your mistake. Once you have prayed for forgiveness and repented for your sin move on and keep striving towards Christ.

Sometimes we do stupid things without thinking first. For example, what do you think Christians seeking to ban the Harry Potter books accomplished? Nothing constructive, that's for sure. In fact, it gave the author and books more attention and increased sales of the books. Making a big deal out of books full of myths, legends and folklore that uses mixed up Latin words as "spells" being cast by cute and friendly little characters, makes you look very ignorant and narrow minded. A fantasy story cannot overcome the power and glory of the Creator of the universe!

Policing what your own children read or are exposed to is an important part of parenting. If you decide a product is not something worthy of your children, don't buy it. Use your consumer dollars to vote on products. If you want Hollywood to make more family friendly movies, pay to go see more family friendly movies and don't economically support the inappropriate movies. This is much more powerful than trying to ban Harry Potter from the library or bookstore.

Do you really want to take away a writer's First Amendment rights in our Constitution? Censoring freedom of speech works both ways. If you censor J.K. Rowling, then she and her readers can seek to ban a Christian author from the library or marketplace. Do you really want censorship in our media? We already have it and the anti-Christians call it "hate speech" and accuse people of "hate crimes". Do you think this overbearing set of laws is good for the preservation of your freedom of religion? "Hate Crimes" are the enforcement arm of political correctness which has already changed the way we speak. We call ourselves Asian-Americans, European-Americans, Native-Americans, or African-Americans. I personally call every U.S. Citizen "Americans" and I am not concerned with what their racial or ethnic background happens to be. Why? Because we are all the children of God, even those who refuse to recognize the fact God exists.

**Job number five** is to not be pushy. Should we be trying to force our beliefs on other people? No. God gave mankind free will. Mankind was given the freedom by God to decide whether or not to believe in Him or to ask Jesus Christ into their hearts. We should only try to influence peoples' thinking in a positive manner. For example at the end of World War Two the defeated Emperor of Japan asked American General Douglas MacArthur how he should convert his people to Christianity. The General replied that Christianity did not work that way. People must be free to decide for themselves whether or not to embrace the Christian faith. America would not force Japan to become a Christian nation.

**Job number six** is to think. God gave us minds to think and ponder about things. Shallow thinking leads to knee jerk reactions that are very unwise. Think through a situation thoroughly and pray for guidance before making a decision. The wisest man ever to live was King Solomon of Israel. He was also the wealthiest person ever. As a Christian Entrepreneur your goal is to create wealth to help your family, your church, your community, and even your nation. Pray for the wisdom of King Solomon. By doing this, you are praying for the ability to think about a situation from all angles including the long term ramifications. Think and pray about how we can make things better for the next generation of Christians in America.

**Job number seven** is to be involved in your community. If you sponsor a cheerleader at the local high school you are helping to make her dream come true. If you sponsor a Little League Baseball Team, you are helping our young people learn about teamwork, individual responsibility, and how to compete with others while being good sports whether they win or lose. By becoming the President of the local Lions Club or a Deacon in your church, you are taking the time to reach out and help others. Sponsor an adoption and help create a new family. These acts and many others are very much a part of being a Christian Entrepreneur.

It is also important to be involved in the good fight to defend our freedom of religion and our faith against those who want to destroy it. Speaking about politics in a church setting is probably not a great idea, because people of many different political parties are Christians. They all try to help people. Some people think the government is the solution to all problems. The problem is politicians are human and governments have a very poor track record when it comes to really helping people. Local churches and national Christian organizations such as The Salvation Army have a much better track record when it comes to helping the poor or hurting. When God is put in control He supernaturally helps and multiplies our efforts.

You as a Christian business leader in the community can talk about politics and help people choose the political candidates that best reflect our Christian values and goals. As a business leader you can and should influence your community in the right political directions to really get results. Words can be pretty, but solid results are what we are all after when it comes to politics. Be careful and very discerning when choosing to back a particular political candidate.

The American Civil Liberties Union, better known as the ACLU, is an anti-Christian organization that must be fought against. This organization has distorted the separation of church and state writings of our Founding Fathers and used this new concept to manipulate our courts. Their goal is to remove Christianity and our influence from our institutions such as schools, the legal system, and all levels of government. The ACLU never sues over the influence of other religions in these places, only Christianity.

To counter the power of the ACLU in our legal system, Christian lawyers have created a legal organization dedicated to fighting the good fight against the ACLU. It is called the Alliance Defense Fund and the website is www.lc.org so that you can go check it out for yourself. This is an organization that deserves your support.

**Job number eight** is to support capitalism as our nation's economic system. The freedom to form pools of capital to help start businesses in America is critical to our survival as a nation. The U.S.A. currently has the number one economy in the world, but we are fading at an alarming speed due to too much government debt combined with too much consumer debt. Social Security and Medicare are paying out more money than the FICA tax is collecting. In other words our two largest government entitlement programs are broke. The only solution is to start as many new businesses as possible—Christ-centered businesses.

Even the Godless Communists in China have learned that capitalism is the number one economic system to grow an economy. So far capitalism has lifted over four hundred million Chinese out of abject poverty in China and they are just getting started. To lift our economy out of its downward spiral, we need to incubate new businesses more than ever to expand the tax base and create new wealth. Wealth is not finite. You can continue to create more wealth in America, but only if the government gets out of the way of the private sector and allows growth. If you want to really help the poor, give them the dignity of a job.

**Job number nine** is to continue to pursue your personal spiritual growth. Reach out to God the Father, Jesus our Savior and the Holy Spirit by being an active Christian. Make Bible study and prayer a part of your daily life. Listen to podcasts of sermons on your MP3 player. Read Christian books and magazines filled with fiction and non-fiction. Listen to Christian radio programs and watch Christian TV programs. Keep learning any way you can.

As you become a more mature Christian you will become more loving towards others and more wise and calm when handling all of life's calamities. You will bear fruit of the Spirit and receive gifts from the Holy Spirit that will help you in your personal ministry. As a Christian business leader you will find fulfillment in your life, because you will be making a positive difference.

## Christian Entrepreneur Profile

Robert Norman Edmiston is a British automotive entrepreneur and the founder of International Motors which acquired the United Kingdom franchises for Subaru and Isuzu cars. Later Edmistion branched out into real estate and auto financing after creating several new businesses under the umbrella of IM Group. His net worth in 2009 was estimated at over 520 million British Pounds.

Edmiston is a Pentecostal Christian who has made large donations to charities which he has established. The most important among these is Christian Vision which he founded in 1993. Christian Vision is a large international evangelical charity with an endowment from Edmiston of 200 million British Pounds. The mission statement of Christian Vision is; "To introduce people to Jesus and encourage those who acknowledge Him to accept Him as the Son of God and become His true followers."

Edmiston also founded two Christian secondary schools within the English academy program—Grace Academy at Coventry and Grace Academy at Solihull. Edmiston is the Chair of Governors for both academies.

## Executive Summary

**Our Purpose**
1. Our purpose is to spread the gospel to the world.
2. Christianity is under attack in the U.S.A.
3. "Hate Speech" and "Hate Crime" laws are being used to limit our freedom of religion and speech.
4. Non-Christians view Christians as; narrow minded, judgmental, anti-science, anti-homosexual, intolerant of other religions, trying to force our beliefs on others, and hypocritical jerks.
5. Christian Entrepreneurs have to walk a fine line.

**Nine Jobs of a Christian Entrepreneur**
Job One = walk the talk
Job Two = offer time for prayer and Bible study at work
Job Three = support charities with Christian values
Job Four = have a sense of humor about yourself and your faith
Job Five = do not be pushy about your faith
Job Six = think things through
Job Seven = be involved in your community
Job Eight = support capitalism to better help the poor
Job Nine = pursue personal spiritual growth

**Christian Entrepreneur Profile**
- Robert Norman Edmiston, the founder of International Motors and Christian Vision.

# Afterword
# The American Dream

**Pursuing the American Dream through Christ**
What is the American Dream to you? When I ask people that question some respond it means to own a home. Others say it is all about the freedom to start your own business. In America we are free to succeed but we are also free to fail. Overcoming failures is part of eventually becoming successful. Achieving the American Dream is not easy, but it is definitely worth it.

In most countries it is very difficult to start a business at all. Government corruption requires payoffs and bribes on top of large fees to get the bureaucracy to approve needed business licenses. There are very few financial mechanisms to capitalize a business. Banks and investors tend to work with only an elite group of potential business founders.

Take Mexico for instance, most of the nation is trapped in the lower class. A small middle class exists, but often works for the government or foreign corporations. A very elite upper class owns most of the land and businesses while controlling the government. This unfortunately is typical in most countries.

When asked most Americans would say the country that most resembles the U.S.A. is the United Kingdom.

Culturally I would agree, but economically the U.K. is a tottering socialist country that is only a shadow of its former greatness as the world's largest empire. A good example of this is the fact that 70% of British subjects rent their homes, while 68% of Americans own their homes. The square footage of a middle class family's home in the U.K. is 905 square feet, while the average middle class home in the U.S.A. is 2001 square feet.

Today America is the #1 economy in the world with a $14 trillion Gross Domestic Product (GDP). China is the newly crowned second largest economy with a GDP of just $1.3 trillion. America's population is around 305 million and China's population is over 1 billion. Japan, with roughly the same population as the U.S.A., has fallen to #3 with a GDP of $1.28 trillion. When I was in college in the early 1980's Japan had the #1 economy in the world and the U.S.A. was in second place.

The lesson to be learned is the American form of capitalism practiced from 1983 to 2007 was the greatest economic engine ever created in the history of the world! At the end of 2008 we slipped backward in the economic policies of Franklin D. Roosevelt and later Jimmy Carter. The result is historically similar high unemployment and slow growth. Hopefully we can turn these bad policies around in the coming years. You can make a difference.

Pursuing the American Dream through Christ is one of the greatest adventures you can possibly experience in your life. The main reason is we serve a living God that is actively involved in our lives if we choose to allow Him to be. By prayerfully asking for business guidance from the Holy Spirit we draw closer to our creator since we begin working with Him on a daily basis.

No matter what you do in life there are some people who are not going to understand and will criticize you and your efforts. That is normal. People are very different from one another. Some wear three piece suits and some wear tie-dye shirts. Individual choices are what Americans enjoy every day, whether they appreciate that freedom or not.

Some people will not like even the thought of pursuing the American Dream through Christ. They can't imagine mixing their religious life with their business life. That is okay. Becoming a Christian Entrepreneur isn't for everybody. Some will shrink away from the idea of drawing close enough to God to actually go into business with Him.

The whole point of starting a Christ-centered business is to become financially strong enough to help others effectively. Results are what counts in business. My definition of success is being able to take care of my family and be able to help fund the Kingdom of God her on earth. You are already a success in the most important decision of free will in your life—you decided to ask Jesus Christ into your heart and then into your business! That is a great example of wisdom in action!

## Aterword
# Bible Study

### Biblical Wisdom

It is important to start every day with some Bible study time. This puts your mind at ease and relieves stress. It keeps you familiar with the voice of God by reading His Word as a matter of habit. This familiarity is extremely important because you need to be able to recognize the voice of the Holy Spirit inside you to help you make the right decisions in your Christ-centered business. The bottom line is the only way to build your Biblical wisdom is to read and study the Word.

This section is not meant to be a complete collection of Bible verses that relate to business but it will help get you started. One of the goals of the Christian Entrepreneur Club website (www.christianentrepreneurclub.com) is to create a subscription based e-newsletter. An important part of that newsletter will be to review a Bible verse with each issue. If you come across a Bible verse that you like and want to share, please email me at brucegmp@yahoo.com and I will try to share it in the newsletter.

### Bible Study

Numerous verses in the Bible inform us that we will be rewarded for adhering to the Word of God. If you believe in the Bible as the Word of God as I do, you should also share my belief that good things happen to those who have faith in the long run.

>Deuteronomy 7:12-13 says, *"If you heed these ordinances, by diligently observing them, the Lord your God will maintain with you the covenant of loyalty that He swore to your ancestors; he will love you, bless you, and multiply you."*

## Ambassadors of Christ

Being a Christian is a 24 hour a day, seven day a week effort to walk the talk. Do I fail sometimes? You bet! As much as I try to mirror Jesus Christ I cannot match Jesus because he was the only perfect man to walk the face of the earth. (Adam was perfect before the fall, so eventually he became an imperfect sinner like those of us that followed later.) That is why I lean on the strength of the Lord to be the best person I can be. In a way we are the representatives of Christ here on earth—we are His ambassadors.

>2 Corinthians 5:20 says, *"So we are ambassadors for Christ, since God is making His appeal through us; we entreat you on behalf of Christ, be reconciled to God."*

## The Blessed have a Mission

When the Lord blesses you with something like your family or a successful business among many other forms of blessings, you have a responsibility to share that blessing with others. Spread the word about your blessing. That doesn't mean brag about something, but it does mean give God the credit.

When I was called by the Holy Spirit to write this book and teach this seminar, my initial reaction was a strong NO! I did not want to stick my neck out and have some Christians and non-believers attack me and my family for taking a stand for my faith. My biggest fear is that members of my own community will send me hate emails for some tiny error in word choice or some other mistake I make. I am only human and unfortunately I am going to keep making mistakes, but overall I am trying my best to help my fellow Christians.

God convicted me that since He had blessed me with the ability to think, write, and verbally express myself in front of people, that it was time for me to use those talents for His glory. This book is the hardest thing I have ever written, but it is worth it if I can help just one person start the next big faith-based business that will help thousands of people.

> Luke 12:48 says, *"From everyone to whom much has been given, much will be required; and from the one to whom much has been entrusted, even more will be demanded."*

## A Giver's Heart

We do not give money or our time in order to receive rewards from God. Having a giver's heart is about following Christ's teachings, not expecting a tangible return on investment. When you mentor someone you give your time and attention to help someone. This is a win/win situation because you always learn something from the person you are mentoring.

Volunteering to coach a youth sports team is a great way to give back to your community. Without volunteers youth sports organizations would not exist and kids would miss out on the experience of being on a sports team. Developing athletic skills and good character in children through sports is very valuable.

> Luke 6:38 says, *"Give, and it will be given to you. A good measure, pressed down, shaken together, running over, will be put into your lap; for the mea-*

*sure you give will be the measure you get back."*

Luke 6:45 says, *"The good person out of the good treasure of the heart produces good, and the evil person out of the evil treasure produces evil; for it is out of the abundance of the heart that the mouth speaks."*

## Building a Good Reputation

We know that God's Word is worth more than all the riches in the world. What is your word worth? Do you do what you say you will do? Can people trust you? Your integrity and reputation are incredibly important in the business world and in your personal life.

Proverbs 22:1 says, *"A good name is to be chosen rather than great riches, and favor is better than silver or gold."*

## Developing Your Staff

When you hire someone you should immediately start developing that person to become a better person and a more valuable employee. It is important for entrepreneurs to delegate work to others to avoid burnout. Employees are the best way to balance out your life and not overwork. You must put some faith in your employees and train them to help you achieve even more success in business. Great businesses blossom through the work of many people working as a team.

Matthew 13:31 says, *"The kingdom of heaven is like a mustard seed that someone took and sowed in his field. It is the smallest of all seeds, but when it has grown it is the greatest of shrubs and becomes a tree."*

## Being Your Best

Only the Lord embodies perfection, but it is important for us to strive for excellence. As a business leader your goal is to excel in the service of people. That means not just customers and employees but also your community and those not directly involved with your business. The satisfaction you feel when you do a good job is a glory we are given from God.

> Psalms 8:3-5 says, *"When I look at your heavens, the work of your fingers, the moon and the stars that you have established; what are human beings that you are mindful of them, mortals that you care for them? Yet you have made them a little lower than God, and crowned them with glory and honor."*

## Staying Positive

If you are a regular consumer of the news you can certainly get caught up in the myriad of problems and issues facing our nation. The old expression is that you can only count on death and taxes. I would add to that the pervasiveness of change. We live in an amazingly ever changing business environment. But by paying too much attention to this world, we can become negative and cynical. It is important to keep your eyes on the Lord and be filled with hope as we work towards a better future.

> Romans 8: 24-25 says, *"For in hope we are saved. Now hope that is seen is not hope. For who hopes for what is seen? But if we hope for what we do not see, we wait for it with patience."*

## Number One

Who or what is number one in your life? Is it football or golf? Is it your business? Is it making money? Christians are taught to put their relationship with God first for a reason. If you are not focused on accomplishing one thing first and foremost, you will fail. The most important priority for us is to serve God. When we get confused about this we find ourselves in trouble.

> Matthew 6:24 says, *"No one can serve two masters."*

## Greatness

When you become a successful business person, you will have many people tell you that you are great. Many today would regard Donald Trump to be a great businessman. (I do not.) What really makes a businessperson great or not great? My first answer would be humility before your creator—God and an attitude of service to all. That is why Truett Cathy, the founder of Chik-fil-A, is in my opinion a great businessman. This same wisdom will make you a great spouse or parent.

> Mark 10:43-45 says, *"...whoever wishes to become great among you must be your servant, and whoever wishes to be first among you must be slave of all. For the Son of Man came not to be served but to serve, and to give His life a ransom for many."*

## Thinking Long Term

A weakness of many modern businesses is short term thinking. Caring only about the next quarterly results is not wise in the long run. Many of today's business failures can be linked to short term thinking rather than planning for long term success. Most businesses do not make a profit until the fourth or even fifth year in business. Amazon did not make a profit in its first seven years of business, but today it is one of the most profitable businesses in the world. It took careful long term planning to make it happen for Amazon.

Developing long-term relationships is essential for any business. This includes relationships with employees, vendors, and customers. Recruiting and training employees is expensive so it is important to maintain a strong relationship with them. Attracting new customers to a business is expensive as well, so it is important to make sure they are satisfied customers that continue to do business with you. Having strong long term relationships with your vendors (suppliers) can mean the difference between success and failure in business. When you have repeat business with the same vendors it can lead to deeper discounts and increased profitability for your business.

Likewise we need to develop a strong long term relationship with the Lord in all aspects of our business and personal lives. This relationship is forever.

> Revelation 1:8 says, *"'I am the Alpha and the Omega,' says the Lord God, who is and who was and is to come, the Almighty."*

## Finding a Niche

Every business must differentiate itself from its competitors. No company can serve everyone in a given marketplace. For example Toyota is the world's largest car manufacturer today, but it cannot serve the needs of everyone who needs a vehicle. Some people need dump trucks or cross-country trucks to haul freight. Toyota does not make those types of vehicles or even work vans. Other manufacturers fill those needs in the marketplace. Large companies in particular cannot serve the needs of smaller niche markets such as Police cars or high-end sports cars.

Not all of your efforts at developing a marketplace are going to bear fruit, but you need to search for an underserved niche. This temporary lack of competition will allow your business to survive the initial start-up costs as you grow your business. In marketing terms you have to let people know what makes your company unique and worthy of their patronage.

> Mark 4:3-8 says, *"A sower went to sow. And as he sowed, some seed fell on the path, and the birds came and ate it up. Other seed fell on rocky ground, where it did not have much soil, and it sprang up quickly, since it had no root, it withered away. Other seed fell among thorns, and the thorns grew up and choked it, and it yielded no grain. Other seed fell into good soil and brought forth grain, growing up and increasing and yielding thirty and sixty and a hundredfold."*

## Standing Firm

Critics are a part of life for those who stand up and try to achieve something special. Standing out from the crowd and doing something different than the majority is guaranteed to garner negative reactions from some. Negativity is easy. Striving to achieve a lofty goal is difficult and challenging. When you declare to the world that you are a Christ-centered business you are going to catch some flack.

Using God's strength and wisdom to weather the storms that happen to every new business is vital for a Christian entrepreneur. Standing firm on your core values and principles as a Christ-centered business is not being stubborn rather it is showing a faith in God. However, there is a fine line between good business planning and testing the Lord by asking Him to make your business successful when you haven't fully thought through your business idea. When you have done your homework properly and paid the dues to gain wisdom do not back down from doing the right thing, even in the face of strong opposition.

> John 15:18-19 says, *"If the world hates you, be aware that it hated me before it hated you. If you*

> belonged to the world, the world would love you as its own. Because you do not belong to the world, but I have chosen you out of the world—therefore the world hates you."

## Solid Business Practices

One of the greatest virtues any business leader can have is being consistent. Being prayerful and thoughtful before making a decision is the only way to make the right decision from the beginning. Sometimes this consistency can only be gained with business experience, but Christian entrepreneurs have an advantage—God as a business partner. Spiritual guidance is the benefit of a humble and prayerful attitude towards our creator.

Providing a consistently high quality service or product to your customers is the only way to succeed in business. If a restaurant chain has some locations serving better quality food than others, eventually the poor service of the few will bring down the entire business. Consistency of purpose leads to business success. Consumers can put their faith in a business that consistently performs well.

> Hebrews 11:1 says, *"Now faith is the assurance of things hoped for, the conviction of things not seen."*

## Creating a Business Team

Lone business mavericks always get overtaken by a strong business team. Soccer is a team sport and so is business. You alone cannot see all of the potential obstacles that your business will face. That is why it is important for you to get feedback from others as you develop your business idea into a business plan.

A Certified Public Accountant (CPA) and a solid business attorney must at the very least be a part of your business team. Women think differently than men, so always get the feedback of the opposite gender when starting a business. By seeking out different points of view, you can gain ideas that you would not have thought of working alone.

> Ecclesiastes 4:9-12 says, *"Two are better than one, because they have a good reward for their toil. For if they fall, one will lift up the other; but woe to one who is alone and falls and does not have another to help. Again, if two lie together, they keep warm; but how can one keep warm alone? And though one might prevail against another, two will withstand one. A threefold cord is not quickly broken."*

> Exodus 18:21 says, *"Find some capable, Godly, honest men who hate bribes, and appoint them as judges, one judge for each 1,000 people, he in turn will have ten judges under him, each in charge of a hundred, and under each of them will be two judges, each responsible for the affairs of fifty people; and each of these will have five judges beneath him, each counseling ten persons."*

## Calculating Risks

Even after doing your homework and writing a well thought out business plan that you believe in, the outcome is not guaranteed. Those who try to predict the future cannot do so with complete accuracy. So an entrepreneur must go with his gut feeling about a potential business. A Christian entrepreneur prays first and goes with what the Holy Spirit tells his gut to feel. Then you have to take that leap of faith and overcome any setbacks that may occur along the way. Learning from your mistakes and refusing to give up makes it all turn out all right.

> John 20:29 says, *"Blessed are those who have*

*not seen and yet have come to believe."*

## The Golden Rule

The Golden Rule is a simple yet great philosophy about how to treat people. It works with employees and customer alike. It's what we do on a daily basis in our Christian businesses to be a customer driven company.

> Matthew 7:12 says, *"In everything do to others as you would have them do to you."*

## Confrontation

In any confrontation it is important to be open and listen to opposing viewpoints. Confrontation is a part of business life, but we must be tolerant and realize confrontation is not necessarily a negative thing. Allowing employees or customers to get out their frustrations or anger can give us as opportunity to listen and grow.

> Matthew 7:1-5 says, *"Do not judge, so that you may not be judged. For with the judgment you make you will be judged, and the measure you give will be the measure you get. Why do you see the speck in your neighbor's eye, but do not notice the log out of your own eye? Or how can you say to your neighbor, 'Let me take the speck out of your eye, while the log is still in your eye? You hypocrite, first take the log out of your own eye, and then you will see clearly to take the speck out of your neighbor's eye."*

> James 1:2-4 says, *"My brothers and sisters, whenever you face trials of any kind, consider it nothing but joy, because you know that the testing of your faith produces endurance, and let it have its full effect, so that you may be mature and complete, lacking in nothing."*

## Abundance

The fact that you have an abundance of wealth is

not a sign of God's blessings. Having a disciplined lifestyle with an abundance of wealth is a better witness to others than the abundance could ever be. An interesting fact is that Christ has more messages in the Bible for the wealthy than for the poor. This reveals that the wealthy have a greater responsibility than the poor.

> 2 Corinthians 8:14 says, *"Your abundance being a supply for their want, that their abundance also may become a supply for your want, that there may be equality."*

## Accountability

Do you listen to the will of the Lord in your life? When you are asked to do something uncomfortable for the Lord, are you obedient? Something that is sorely lacking among American Christians these days is accountability. Violating God's principles in the areas of personal and business finance leads to the type of ruin that we are currently experiencing. God has laid out guiding principles for us to follow. If we refuse to learn and follow these teachings God is not responsible to bail us out. He has specifically warned us to avoid debt in the first place. Now God is benevolent and sometimes He does bail us out, but it is wise to not test the Lord. Since God is the absolute authority in our lives it is important for us to obey His lessons.

> Luke 6:46 says, *"Why do you call Me 'Lord, Lord' and do not do what I say?"*

## Vision and Planning

To be an effective Christian business leader you must have a vision of where you want to take your company. Without a plan to follow in business, nothing gets done. Write your vision down in a business plan to spell out what your business goals are and how you intend to achieve them. Share this plan with your employees and investors to gain their feedback. Meaningful visions usually come when you are quiet and at peace. Prayer time can be a time when the Holy Spirit communicates visions to you that will help your business.

A vision causes a light bulb to go off with a great idea. A brainstorm of thinking usually follows that initial vision and helps solidify the idea into something that can become reality. Remember when you fill a need that other's have you are creating a successful business. Wealth will follow when you have discovered a way to help others.

> Habakkuk 2:2 says, *"Write the vision and make it plain on tablets, so that he may run who reads it."*

> Matthew 6:33 says, *"But strive first for the kingdom of God, and His righteousness, and all these things will be given to you as well."*

> Proverbs 22:3 says, *"A prudent man foresees the difficulties ahead and prepares for them; the simpleton goes blindly on and suffers the consequences."*

> Proverbs 24:3-4 says, *"Any enterprise is built by wise planning, becomes strong through common sense, and profits wonderfully by keeping abreast of the facts."*

> Luke 14:28 says, *"But don't begin until you count the cost. For who would begin construction of a building without first getting estimates and then checking to see if he has enough money to pay the bills?"*

> Proverbs 16:3 says, *"Commit to the Lord whatever you do, and your plans will succeed."*

> Proverbs 29:18 says, *"Where there is no vision, the people perish: but he that keeps the law is happy.*

## The Rock

Build your business on the rock of Christ's teachings. In order to build a tall building an engineer needs a firm foundation planted deep in the ground. The same is true of a business. The strongest foundation for a business is the truth found in the Bible and a solid relationship with God. If you plant seeds wisely in the beginning of a venture, you will be reap the rewards times a hundred in the future. The Word of God is like a river of water that sustains us.

> Jeremiah 17:8 says, *"They shall be like a tree planted by water, sending out its roots by the stream. It shall not fear when heat comes, and its leaves shall stay green; in the year of drought it is not anxious, and it does not cease to bear fruit."*

## Accumulation

Wealth is the side effect of serving others well in business. Unless a business is a faith-based business it will not have an eternal impact. That business will eventually wither and die and become like dust in a strong wind. All that truly matters is what we can do for the kingdom of God. Accumulating material things is not important. Material things are mere tools that we use to accomplish God's work. All things flow from God, so they are really His in the first place. He graciously lets us borrow them for a short time during our lives here on earth.

The Bible warns us that the accumulation of wealth is a major obstacle to maintaining a humble spirit. Money can cause us to want to be served instead of serving others. Hubris has been the downfall of many people the world thought were great individuals. With God as your business partner, you can't take full credit for your successes.

Matthew 20:26-28 says, *"Whomever wishes to become great among you shall be your servant, and whoever wishes to be first among you shall be your slave; just as the Son of Man did not come to be served, but to serve, and to give His life a ransom for many."*

## Tough Times

We are not meant to live a life without adversity. Troubles are a part of life. God's plan for creating strong disciples involves some challenges. This is necessary in order to mature us spiritually. No matter what happens to us, the Lord wants us to trust Him fully. God may use your bad situation as a testimony for others or to reinforce a lesson.

When I was twenty-three years old my father called to inform me that my mother had died earlier that day in a small plane crash. The news devastated our family. My mother was the person who had held us together. Without her presence we fell apart as a family. My mother was a wonderful Christian woman. Why would God allow such a horrible death to happen to such a beloved person? We were all asking that same question.

My father and I grew closer to God over time and eventually reconciled our relationship. My siblings renounced Christ and ran away from God. To this day my family is spiritually split. Trusting God is not easy after such an event, but He knew it was my mother's time to go home at age fifty-two. I do know that many people were influenced by her to accept Christ. With the writing of this book I have come full circle in my walk with Christ.

Psalm 34:19 says, *"Many are the afflictions of the righteous: but the Lord delivers him out of them all."*

## Fear and Anxiety

Providing for a family can produce some moments of shear anxiety. I sometimes suffer from anxiety attacks in the middle of the night for no logical reason. Debt can create anxiety and fear of failure which is why it is best to avoid personal debt. Seeking God through prayer time and Bible study is the best way I know to overcome anxiety and fear of failure.

When you have financial responsibilities it is okay to pray for God's help to fill the needs of your family. God always answers prayers. However we don't always get the answers we want at the time we want them. God's timing and purpose does not always match our own. Realizing these facts is part of maturing as a Christian.

Philippians 4:6 says, *"Be anxious for nothing, but in everything by prayer and supplication with thanksgiving let your requests be made known to God."*

## Mission Statement

Every business needs a mission statement to succinctly summarize the purpose of the business. The mission statement of my website ChristianEntrepreneurClub.com is as follows;

"To help build the kingdom of God here on earth — one Christ-centered business at a time."

The mission statement of Jesus Christ is found in Matthew 5:3-12 which says, "Blessed are the poor in spirit, for theirs is the kingdom of heaven. Blessed are those who mourn, for they will be comforted. Blessed are the meek, for they will inherit the earth. Blessed are those who hunger and thirst for righteousness, for they will be filled. Blessed are the merciful, for they will receive mercy. Blessed are the pure in heart, for they will see God. Blessed are the peacemakers, for they will be called children of God. Blessed are you when people revile you and persecute you and utter all kinds of evil against you falsely on my account. Rejoice and be glad, for your reward is great in heaven, for in the same way they persecuted the prophets who were before you."

The mission statement of Christianity is known as the Great Commission which is found in Matthew 28:19 "Go therefore and make disciples of all nations, baptizing them in the name of the Father and the Son and the Holy Spirit."

**Good Steward**

All things flow from God who is the actual owner. We are not business owners. Instead we are business managers or stewards. The Lord will entrust us with His wealth, but he expects us to manage it carefully for him. Our attitude is what is important to God. He wants to bless and prosper His people according to His will for their individual lives. Americans have grown arrogant and become poor stewards of the wealth of our nation. If we Christian entrepreneurs don't help turn this around, America will self-destruct.

> Luke 12:42 says, *"The Lord said, 'Who then is the faithful and sensible steward, whom his master will put in charge of his servants to give them their rations at the proper time?"*
>
> 1 Timothy 3:4-5 says, *"He must be one who manages his own household well, keeping his children under control with all dignity. But if a man does not know how to manage his own household, how will he take care of the church of God?"*

**Changing Your Heart**

It is always possible to change your heart and draw closer to God. The Lord is very forgiving of your sins as long as you move away from those transgressions (repent). No matter how hard we try to not disappoint God we will make mistakes. If you fall away from your church community, your family, and your faith it is never too late to turn your life around. Only Christianity among the religions of the world offers redemption and forgiveness that is absolute and given by God in the form of unconditional love.

> Psalm 119:58-60 says, *"With all my heart I want Your blessings. Be merciful just as You promised. I thought about the wrong direction in which I was headed, and turned around and came running back to You."*

## Meditate on the Word

Rejoice in the fact that our God has inspired His disciples to write down His Holy Word. Truth is truth no matter when it was actually written down and the Bible is full of truth that will help you run a business. Obstacles occur every day in business, so it is important to meditate on the Word every single day, not just on Sundays.

> Psalm 119:12, 15,-16 says, *"Praise be to you, O Lord...I meditate on your precepts and consider your ways. I delight in your decrees; I will not neglect your word."*

## Paying your Bills

If you can pay a bill you legitimately owe you should go ahead and do so. Withholding money from people who have extended you credit is not okay with God. Filing for bankruptcy is not okay with God either. Bankruptcy is a no win situation. It damages your credit for ten years. Dave Ramsey and Clark Howard are two personal financial gurus that I listen to every week. Both gentlemen say it is better to contact your creditors and work out a new written agreement with them to pay back your debt. This approach only takes five years to transform your situation back to good credit.

> Proverbs 3:27 says, *"Don't withhold repayment of your debts. Don't say 'some other time' if you can pay now."*

## Charity

Helping fellow Christians in need and showing hospitality to strangers is a basic part of being a Christian. As a member of a local church you should be able to look to the fellowship as an extension of God's provision. In other words, if you hit a tough time in your life your church family should be there to help you. Likewise when someone in your church is hurting they should be able to count on you and other church members for help. Christian charity also extends outside of our faith as a way of attracting unbelievers to our religion.

> James 2:15-16 says, *"If you have a friend who is in need of food and clothing, and you say to him, 'Well, good-bye and God bless you; stay warm and eat hearty,' and then don't give him clothes or food, what good does that do?"*

## Spiritual Reward

Each of us has an economic destiny. As the children of God we are supposed to be a contributing member of His covenant in our local churches here on earth. God wants His children to live in abundance, not poverty, so that we can give Him the credit and go help those in trouble. All we have to do is be obedient to God's teachings about being a good steward. That is the tricky part. We tend to mess up when it comes to being obedient. It is hard for us to not follow our free will, die unto ourselves and follow Christ's teachings completely. The more we are obedient, the more we are rewarded spiritually.

Deuteronomy 8:18 says, *"But you shall remember the Lord your God for it is He that gives you power to get wealth, that He may establish His covenant which He swore with your fathers as it is this day."*

Psalm 37:25 says, *"I have been young and now I am old; yet I have not seen the righteous forsaken, nor His seed begging bread."*

3 John 2 says, *"Beloved, I wish above all things that you may prosper and be in health, even as your soul prospers."*

Proverbs 13:22 says, *"The wealth of the sinner is laid up for the just."*

Proverbs 10:22 says, *"The blessing of the Lord, it makes you rich, and He adds no sorrow with it."*

Psalm 35:27 says, *"Let the Lord be magnified, which has pleasure in the prosperity of His servant."*

Luke 19:17 says, *"'Well done my good servant,' his master replied. 'Because you have been trustworthy in a very small matter, take charge of ten cities.'"*

## The Importance of Knowledge

A reason why so many Christians seem to be struggling financially today is their lack of knowledge about what the Word of God has to say about finances. That is why books and seminars like this exist today. This is also the reason why I was led to include this Bible Study section in this book.

Hosea 4:6 says, *"My people are destroyed for lack of knowledge."*

Genesis 24:34-35 says, *"So he said, 'I am Abraham's servant. The Lord has blessed my master abundantly, and he has become wealthy. He has given him sheep and cattle, silver and gold, menservants and maidservants, and camels and donkeys.'"*

## Make an Honest Profit

We are in business to make an honest profit, not to cheat or steal from anyone. One unhappy customer can create a word of mouth campaign against your company that can destroy it—especially in the age of the Internet. Christian entrepreneurs are not greedy or dishonest. That is why Christian entrepreneurs are so vitally needed to help turn our economy and country around. Our nation needs to move closer to God and His wisdom to avoid being destroyed.

> Matthew 25:28-30 says, *"'Therefore take away the talent (money) from him and give it to the one who has ten talents. For to everyone who has shall be more given, and he shall have abundance; but from the one who does not have even what he does have shall be taken away. And cast out the unprofitable servant into the outer darkness; in that place there shall be weeping and gnashing of teeth."*

## Rich get Richer, while Poor get Poorer

The spirit of poverty seems to affect many Christians. We have our role to play in applying God's principles of finance to our personal and business lives. We must become knowledgeable about Biblical laws of increasing and multiplying wealth. Then we must apply that knowledge in our daily lives. It seems unfair that some people continue to build wealth no matter what the economy is doing, while the poor seem to only get poorer.

God created the universe which operates under certain laws that He established. The law of gravity is part of our everyday existence and we take it for granted. God also put into place laws of money into place here on earth. Once these laws are understood, they will work for believers and even unbelievers just like the law of gravity.

God's law of money is the better you manage your money, the more money you receive. Managing money is being a good steward. Conversely, if you do not manage your money properly, the funds that you do have will never be enough. Eventually, they will be taken away from you. The rich are getting richer because they understand the principles that govern the building of wealth and they manage those principles in their favor.

> Luke 4:18 says, *"The Spirit of the Lord is upon Me. Because He anointed Me to preach the gospel, to the poor. He has sent Me to proclaim release to the captives and recovery of sight to the blind. To set free those who are downtrodden."*
>
> Philippians 4:19 says, *"But my God shall supply all your need according to His riches in glory by Christ Jesus."*
>
> Luke 16:11 says, *"So if you have not been trustworthy in handling worldly wealth, who will trust you with true riches?"*
>
> Matthew 25:21 says, *"His master said to him, 'Well done my good and faithful servant, you have been faithful over a few things, I will make you ruler over many things, enter into the joy of the Lord.'"*

## Humility

A problem many of us have when we achieve financial and business success is that we lose touch with how we got there. Our actions alone do not create wealth. Our understanding and obedience to God's principles of money and our effectively we applied those rules to our business made all the difference. God has the power, we are the tool. It is important to keep our relationship with God in perspective.

> Deuteronomy 8:17-18 says, *"Do not say to your-*

> self, 'My power and the might of my own hand has gotten me this wealth.' But remember the Lord your God for it is He who gives you power to get wealth, so that He may confirm His covenant that He swore to your ancestors, as He is doing today."

## Innovation

God gave us a huge gift—our brains. Not only are we created in His image, we are endowed with the ability to think and create new things. Innovating new products and services and creating new businesses to deliver these through is what makes us special. Animals cannot do these things no matter what PETA says. Trees cannot do these things no matter what environmentalists say. Animals and plants lack a soul and a higher calling from God. Unbelievers try to equivocate animals and "mother earth" to mankind, but only mankind has a creative spark from God.

> Ephesians 3:20-21 says, *"Now to him who by the power at work within us is able to accomplish abundantly far more than all we can ask or imagine, to Him be the glory in the church and in Christ Jesus to all generations forever and ever. Amen."*

## Get Pumped!

Enthusiasm is contagious. Hollow enthusiasm is just noise, but we Christians truly have something to be fired up about. We serve a living God! Jesus overcame death on the cross. We are empowered by the Holy Spirit to accomplish great things. With our faith alone in God we can move mountains. How can anyone who knows Christ be lukewarm in their faith? God asks the same question and adds a warning.

> Revelation 3:15-16 says, *"I know your works; you are neither cold nor hot. I wish that you were either cold or hot. So, because you are lukewarm, and nei-*

*ther cold nor hot, I am about to spit you out of my mouth."*

## The Bondage of Borrowing

Many types of businesses can be started without borrowing. As you design your business idea and then write your business plan, you can be saving up money to launch your business. Sometimes it takes years to properly plan a new business. It is very important to not personally sign for debt when you are starting a new business.

If you need a large sum of money to start a business, you should add investors (Angel investors) into the ownership of the business. You can also offer the sale of stock to the general public which is known as an Initial Public Offering (IPO). You can personally invest in the IPO of stock at the beginning of the venture. Be careful when borrowing money in the name of the business as well, since this can add additional stress and pressures to running your business.

> Matthew 5:25-26 says, *"Come to terms quickly with your enemy before it is too late and he drags you into court and you are thrown into a debtor's cell, for you will stay there until you have paid the last penny."*
>
> Proverbs 22:7 says, *"The rich rule over the poor, and the borrower becomes the lender's slave."*
>
> 1 John 2:15-16 says, *"Love not the world, neither the things that are in the world. If any man loves the world, the love of the Father is not in him. For all that is in the world, the lust of the flesh, and the lust of the eyes, and the pride of life, is not of the Father, but is of the world."*

CPSIA information can be obtained at www.ICGtesting.com
Printed in the USA
LVOW050513280712

291948LV00001B/181/P